Getting to Grips with GNVQs

A

HANDBOOK

FOR

TEACHERS

Geoff Hayward

KOGAN PAGE

First published in 1995

Kogan Page Limited
120 Pentonville Road
London N1 9JN

British Library Cataloguing in Publication Data

A CIP record for this book is available from the British Library.

ISBN 0 7494 1421 9

Typeset by Saxon Graphics Ltd, Derby
Printed in England by Clays Ltd, St Ives plc

Getting to Grips with GNVOs

Contents

Introduction 7

THEME 1 GNVQ BASICS 11

1. The GNVQ model: an overview 13

1.1 What is a GNVQ? 14
1.2 The structure of GNVQs 16
1.3 The function of different types of unit 17
1.4 Inside a GNVQ unit 21
1.5 Roles and responsibilities 26
1.6 Thinking about teaching GNVQs 28

2. Getting started with teaching GNVQs 30

2.1 Preliminary thinking 31
2.2 Reading the elements 32
2.3 Implications for teaching 34
2.4 Underpinning knowledge and understanding 38
2.5 Further implications for teaching 46

3. Assessing GNVQs 49

3.1 An overview of GNVQ assessment 50
3.2 Evidence 52
3.3 Internal continuous assessment 56
3.4 Case study of assessment 58
3.5 Grading 70

4. Writing assignments and controlling paper 79

4.1 Writing assignments 79
4.2 Managing the paper chase: initial steps 83

THEME 2: CORE SKILLS 87

5. Introducing GNVQ core skills 89

5.1 Getting to know the units: a strategy 89
5.2 Specification of core skills 90
5.3 Knowledge, understanding and GNVQ core skills 92

5.4 What core skills do students have to do? 95
5.5 Course delivery 97
5.6 Case studies 99

6. The mandatory core skill units 102

6.1 Communication unit 102
6.2 Application of number 114
6.3 Information technology 121
6.4 Integrating the mandatory core skills with vocational units 125

7. Teaching, learning and assessing core skills 128

7.1 Essential resources 129
7.2 Building a programme 130
7.3 Transferability 134
7.4 Assessing core skills 137

THEME 3: THE MANAGEMENT OF STUDENT LEARNING 143

8. Managing student learning: models and systems 145

8.1 The FEU model 145
8.2 The personal tutor 148
8.3 Running review sessions 150
8.4 Case studies 151

9. Student enrolment and pre-course counselling 156

9.1 Who are GNVQ students? 156
9.2 Sorting students 158
9.3 Pre-enrolment counselling 162
9.4 Pre-enrolment counselling: a case study 163

10. Induction and Action Planning 167

10.1 Induction: what you have to do 167
10.2 Models of induction 172
10.3 Action planning: advice from awarding bodies 175
10.4 Action planning: case studies 178

Bibliography 188

Index 189

Introduction

General National Vocational Qualifications (GNVQs) were introduced in direct response to the Government White Paper, 'Education and Training for the 21st Century', published in May 1991, which called for:

> the development of more general NVQs as an important priority. It [the Government] believes that the NCVQ [National Council for Vocational Qualifications] as a matter of urgency should work with others, including awarding bodies, industry lead bodies and the Further Education Unit, to develop criteria for accrediting more general vocational qualifications. (DES (1991) p18)

To achieve this aim the White Paper set out the following specification:

> General NVQs should cover broad occupational areas, and offer opportunities to develop relevant knowledge and understanding, and to gain an appreciation of how to apply them at work. General NVQs should also:
>
> - offer a broad preparation for employment as well as an accepted route to higher level qualifications, including higher education;
> - require the demonstration of a range of skills and the application of knowledge and understanding relevant to the related occupations;
> - be of equal standing with academic qualifications at the same level;
> - be clearly related to the occupational specific NVQs so that young people can progress quickly and effectively from one to the other;
> - be sufficiently distinct from occupationally specific NVQs to ensure that there is no confusion between the two;
> - be suitable for use by full time students in colleges, and, if appropriate in schools, who have limited opportunities to demonstrate competence in the workplace. (DES (1991) p19)

The Government's intention in the White Paper was clear: to establish a triple track of educational provision within which GNVQ would stand as being equivalent to more traditional qualifications like GCSE and A level and would give access to both Higher Education, the World of Work and further training within the NVQ framework. To help promote parity of esteem with 'academic' qualifications like A level and GCSE, GNVQs were renamed in 1993 as Foundation (Level 1), Intermediate (Level 2) and Advanced (Level 3) GNVQs. This led to the label of 'Vocational A level' being attached to Advanced GNVQ by politicians and the press to emphasise the intention of producing a vocational award at Level 3: '... specifically designed to meet a standard comparable to A and AS level qualifications.' (NCVQ (1993a) p5).

The National Council of Vocational Qualifications (NCVQ) responded rapidly to the Government's request so that by September 1992, just over one year after the publication of the White Paper, GNVQ pilots in five areas, Art and Design, Business, Health and Social Care, Leisure and Tourism and Manufacturing, started. These were to be followed by a further nine GNVQs to be phased in by 1995–6. Currently no further GNVQs are to be developed and introduced after that date.

The initial stages of the 1992 pilots led to many of the qualification specifications being extensively rewritten in the spring of 1993 with accompanying small changes in assessment procedures and advice to centres. This pattern is being repeated for the 1993 pilots with rewriting in 1994 and is likely to be a feature of the development of all GNVQs. Despite these initial teething problems GNVQs have proven to be popular with both students and teachers and despite some criticism, for example by Professor Alan Smithers, they are undoubtedly here to stay.

Whilst it is likely that there will be further evolution in the general shape and scope of the qualification the central ideas, largely but not wholly derived from the National Vocational Qualifications established in the 1980s, especially the concept of demonstrating competence to achieve the award, will remain. Consequently whilst there may be small changes within specific GNVQs these changes are unlikely to affect the sorts of ways that teachers need to think about the teaching of GNVQs. Such tasks as planning the course, inducting students, teaching and learning strategies and methods of assessment are generic to all GNVQs. It is the strategic thinking you need to undertake to accomplish these tasks, and so run a GNVQ course effectively and efficiently, that this book aims to help you with, rather than the specific details of individual courses.

GNVQs are young qualifications and teachers are still developing ways of working within this very new framework. None the less considerable expertise has been developed and this has been reported on within evaluation and research projects run or sponsored by, for example, OFSTED (Office for Standards in Education), FEU (Further Education Unit) and the Departments of Employment (DoE) and Education (DfE). There are also useful information notes available from NCVQ and all three awarding bodies provide booklets of advice to centres, though these do differ.

However, much of this material is not readily accessible, runs to many thousands of pages and may not contain the sort of concrete details which teachers find helpful. So whilst it would be useful to any teacher grappling with a GNVQ course it is difficult to access and use. One of the aims of this book is therefore to draw together at least some of this material to illustrate how different institutions are going about delivering GNVQ. Rather than delivering this in a piecemeal, case-study way, concentrating on one institution at a time, I have tried to use the material to illustrate more general themes in the planning and execution of GNVQs. My intention in doing this is to enable you to use this book in ways which are of direct benefit to you rather than trying to match your institution and situation to a particular case study which you could copy.

One of the main messages which has emerged from the research on existing GNVQ centres is that there is no one way to do a GNVQ. Centres and individual teachers have been able to work flexibly within the qualification framework to provide courses which meet the needs of their students and local conditions. This has led to the development of courses which differ significantly from centre to centre in their emphasis and in the materials they use. Partly this was inevitable: there were simply no teaching materials or published textbooks available in the early days, though this is now being remedied. However, teachers have generally welcomed the freedom to plan courses and devise teaching materials within the general framework of GNVQ whilst recognising the strain this has placed on them. It will be for you to judge and decide the extent to which you develop bespoke materials and approaches or rely on published schemes, though I suspect you will want to adapt the latter to suit your purposes.

The implications for the writing of this book of the research and evaluation projects mentioned above, combined with my own experience of working with teachers and lecturers delivering GNVQ courses, were obvious: I should neither pretend nor suggest there are glib answers or simple solutions to preparing and run a GNVQ course. Rather I have tried to write something which will support, help and guide your thinking without telling you exactly what to do. Such a prescriptive approach would be impossible since what works in one institution will not work in another where conditions of funding, staffing and ways of working are different. There is, however, no point in reinventing the wheel, so if, for example, you are embarked on a strategy for implementing GNVQ which this book indicates has not worked well in another institution then it may, perhaps, suggest a need to think through your plans again. I also hope the ideas and examples given will help to guide you to solutions for problems which you are finding difficult whilst making you aware of issues which you may not even have thought about but which have proven to be problematic in other institutions.

The material has been written for use by individuals within a course team since research on the pilot centres suggests that such a team approach, particularly in the support and reduction in stress that such a team offers to its members, is essential to running a successful GNVQ programme. However, the book will be still be of use if you are working in isolation, if only as a means of helping you to apply leverage to senior managers to foster a team approach in the delivery of GNVQ. The materials are arranged in an order which I think that anybody planning a GNVQ course would have to work through before starting. However, you do not have to use them in this order. Indeed I have deliberately set out to write something which is a manual rather than a book, something which you can dip into if you are already an experienced practitioner and you just want to think about a particular issue. If you are completely new to GNVQ you may want to work through entire chapters or even the whole manual in sequence.

My abiding impression of talking with GNVQ teachers was one of dedicated professionals who were struggling to come to grips with the new demands, both intellectual and practical, being placed on them by GNVQ. For many this has involved a fundamental reappraisal of their thinking about teaching and learning, and ways of working with students who had often not enjoyed great success in their education to date. Their reward was seeing young people achieving and growing in self esteem and confidence by being involved with these new courses. You will not find developing your GNVQ course easy, though I hope this book will help, but I am sure you will reap the same rewards. Good luck!

Theme 1:

GNVQ basics

General National Vocational Qualifications are immensely complicated qualifications. To really understand them and work with them effectively you need to keep several ideas in your head at the same time. This becomes possible as you gain in confidence and experience. However, to begin with what you need is a general sketch, an overview of how GNVQs work and then a more detailed explanation of how the vocational units are constructed and assessed. This will help to identify the constraints that you need to take into account when you are planning to teach GNVQ. This is the purpose of this first theme. If by the time you have completed it you feel confident enough to write your first GNVQ assignment and do not feel you are taking a gigantic step into the dark then these four chapters will have done their job. Once you are confidently working within this small compass you can begin to add additional elements to your thinking about GNVQ: core skills (Theme 2) and the management of student learning (Theme 3).

Do not think you will become an expert at teaching and assessing GNVQ overnight. You won't. It seems to take between six months and a year of working with the courses to develop the feel for them and to gain the experience necessary to assess with confidence. Take advantage of as many INSET opportunities as possible and get yourself signed up for the assessor training. When done well it really helps you to understand GNVQ assessment.

Chapter 1

The GNVQ Model: An Overview

Current experience suggests that effective delivery of GNVQ requires that everyone involved, students and teachers, understand how the qualification works:

> teachers have had to work hard at understanding the structure of GNVQ. This has been an essential first step; a starting point for an understanding of the culture within which GNVQ operates and a basis for planning GNVQ delivery. (Department of Employment (1993) Management p1)

This means that even though you may be responsible for delivering only a small part of a particular GNVQ, say one or two units, you do need to develop an appreciation of the overall structure of a GNVQ, if only to discuss sensibly with your students and colleagues what they and you are doing.

In addition, General National Vocational Qualifications are very different to other qualifications. This uniqueness has proved to be problematic for teachers new to GNVQ who, understandably, have wanted to interpret the structure, teaching and assessment of GNVQ by comparing it with, say, A level, GCSE, CPVE or BTEC National Diploma.

> Probably the clearest message to have emerged from the first two terms of GNVQ was 'GNVQ is different to other current qualifications', most notably in the way it is presented and assessed, and as a consequence of this in the ways it needs to be managed and delivered (Department of Employment (1993) Management p1)

> It is all to easy to see GNVQ as another CPVE ... Indeed, on occasion, previous experience of vocational provision can be a hindrance. (Department of Employment (1993) Management p1)

The purpose of this chapter is, therefore, twofold. Firstly to introduce you to GNVQs and to help you to develop an overview of the structure of the qualification. Secondly to help you understand how GNVQs differ from other qualifications. In particular, I hope it will help you to realise that teaching on a GNVQ will require new thinking and developing new ways of working. Experience from centres currently running GNVQ suggests that developing these new approaches takes time but is helped by adopting team approaches to the delivery of GNVQ programmes.

KEY IDEA: GNVQs require new thinking about teaching and learning combined with new ways of working.

1.1 WHAT IS A GNVQ?

GNVQs are part of an emerging post-16 National Framework of qualifications. Figure 1.1 shows the three main routes or tracks which students can follow within this framework which will, eventually, absorb all post-16 qualifications. Figure 1.1 also indicates that GNVQs aim at a double destination: either into employment or into further or higher education. The employment outcome of GNVQ has been under-emphasised: a GNVQ should prepare a student to benefit from training within the NVQ framework at work in addition to opening up further education possibilities. This point is emphasised by the awarding bodies:

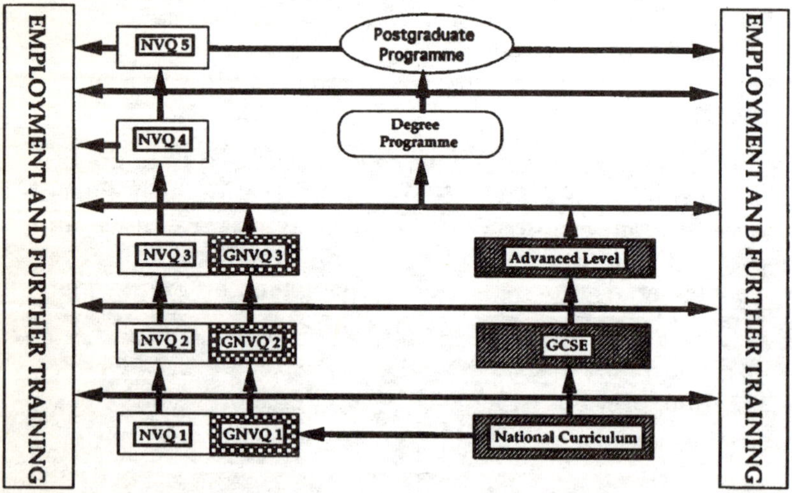

Figure 1.1 *The triple pathway in English and Welsh post-16 education and training. Note the NVQ, GNVQ and so-called academic pathways based on GCSE and A level. Notice how students should be able to transfer between routes.*

> GNVQs have been designed to provide a broad education as a foundation both for training leading to employment, and for further and higher education. This is achieved by ensuring that learners develop the general skills, knowledge and understanding which underpin a wide range of occupations or professions ... (Royal Society of Arts (1993b) p3)

The main point to remember at this stage is that GNVQs are supposed to provide young people with a good general education. They are not limited to providing narrow, job-specific training. This is a confusion which has occurred because GNVQs have evolved from National Vocational Qualifications (NVQs) which are more job-specific qualifications. Whilst GNVQs and NVQs do share some features they differ in significant ways (Table 1.1).

Table 1.1 *A comparison of the main differences between National Vocational Qualifications (NVQs) and General National Vocational Qualifications (GNVQs)*

NVQs	GNVQs
national standards for occupational competence	national standards for broad-based vocational education
standards developed by industry-led bodies	standards developed by NCVQ and awarding bodies
standards set for specific employment functions	standards set for broad vocational areas
assessment of competence	assessment of achievement
units generally vary in size and number at given level	units of equal size and number at given level
a wide number of awards available in each occupational area	limited number of awards available

Who awards GNVQs?

GNVQs are currently awarded by three **awarding bodies:** Business & Technology Education Council (BTEC), City & Guilds of London Institute (CGLI), and the Royal Society of Arts (RSA) Examinations Board. The National Council for Vocational Qualifications (NCVQ) acts as the quality-enforcing body. So whilst NCVQ must give approval for every GNVQ, and every unit offered within a GNVQ, it is not directly involved in the assessment process.

KEY IDEA: Centres offering GNVQs work with one or more awarding bodies not directly with NCVQ.

1.2 THE STRUCTURE OF GNVQs

GNVQs are unit-based qualifications. Each unit in a qualification is designed to be of equal size or challenge to all the other units. Students accumulate credit obtained for each unit until sufficient credits have been accumulated for the student to be awarded the complete qualification.

There are three levels of award currently available: Foundation (Level 1), Intermediate (Level 2) and Advanced (Level 3). Different levels of award make different demands upon students, require different numbers of unit credits and are deemed to have equivalence with qualifications in the other routes within the National framework (Table 1.2).

Table 1.2 *The numbers of units in each type of GNVQ currently available*

Level of award	Number of mandatory vocational units	Number of optional vocational units	Number of core skill units	Equivalent to
Foundation	3	3	3	
Intermediate	4	2	3	Four GCSEs (Grade C)
Advanced	8	4	3	Two A levels

Types of GNVQ unit

Again experience suggests that this is a source of confusion for teachers, especially if they are only involved in teaching a small part of a GNVQ. Figure 1.2 shows the different types of GNVQ unit. Notice that there are

- essentially two types of GNVQ unit: vocational and core skill units.
- three types of vocational unit: Mandatory, Optional and Additional.
- two types of core skill unit: Mandatory and Additional.

Unit Type	Mandatory	Optional	Additional
Vocational	*	*	*
Core Skill	*		*

Figure 1.2 *Different sorts of units available in GNVQs.*

KEY IDEA: UNIT: A unit is the smallest part of a GNVQ qualification that can be certificated. There are two types of unit: vocational units and core skill units. Individual GNVQ units are not graded but the complete award is.

To be awarded a GNVQ students must pass:

- a specified number of mandatory vocational and optional vocational units. The number varies with the level of the award (Table 1.2).
- three mandatory core skill units: Communication, Application of Number and Application of Information Technology.

For example, the award of an Intermediate GNVQ requires a candidate to complete nine units – four mandatory vocational, two optional vocational and three mandatory core skill units (Figure 1.3b). For the award of an Advanced GNVQ a candidate must complete 15 units – eight mandatory vocational units, four optional vocational units and the three mandatory core skill units (Figure 1.3c). The vocational units must be at the level needed for the award, e.g. Advanced units for the Advanced award, and they must be drawn from the same GNVQ.

1.3 THE FUNCTION OF DIFFERENT TYPES OF UNIT

Mandatory vocational units are designed to provide a basic understanding of the scale and scope of a particular vocational area. The optional units allow students to build on this basic knowledge and understanding.

Mandatory vocational units are the same within a GNVQ with the same title and level, irrespective of the awarding body offering the GNVQ. For example Unit 1 in the Intermediate Leisure and Tourism GNVQ is called Investigating Leisure and Tourism (Intermediate) by all the awarding bodies and the content is identical in each case.

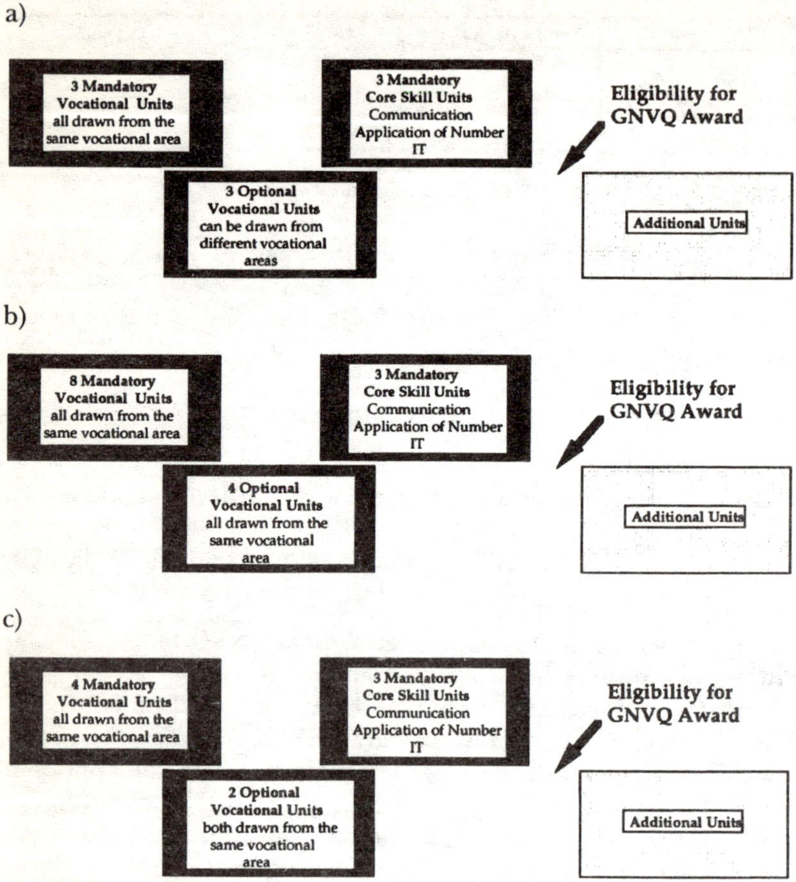

Figure 1.3 *The structure of GNVQs at three different levels. Notice that in each case certain units are compulsory, heavy shading. Notice also the choice of optional units in Foundation GNVQ compared with the other two. (a) Foundation; (b) Intermediate; (c) Advanced.*

Mandatory units do not have to be taught in the order they are listed nor do they have to be taught separately:

> Although units are specified independently learning activities will frequently produce evidence which can be assessed against the specifications of more than one unit. The units do not have to be covered in any particular sequence. (BTEC (1993b) p1)

KEY IDEA: Practically all mandatory units are assessed by a combination of continuous assessment and an externally set test.

Optional units vary between awarding bodies. If you have the opportunity you may, therefore, want to look at the optional GNVQ units available from different awarding bodies and choose the awarding body which offers what you consider to be the best optional units. It is more likely though that your Institution will already have decided which awarding body to work with, in which case you have to use that body's optional units.

Since the challenge of an optional unit is the same as a mandatory or core skill unit this means that you do not have to teach the mandatory units before you teach the optional units. Indeed there may be advantages in integrating the delivery of optional and mandatory units.

KEY IDEA: Optional units are assessed by a combination of continuous assessment and appropriate internal testing.

Additional units allow students to increase the scope and range of their GNVQ. Additional units could include further optional GNVQ units, NVQ units, GCSEs, AS levels or an A level. Additional GNVQ units can be drawn from the optional bank within a particular award or may be drawn from another GNVQ. For example, science students wishing to strengthen their physics could take additional units with a physics base drawn from the option bank for the GNVQ in science. Alternatively the same students could draw upon a unit from the Advanced Business GNVQ. Whilst this may benefit the students, and would certainly fit in with the philosophy of GNVQs, in practice it raises issues of flexible timetabling and resourcing of GNVQ courses which need to be dealt with by senior management.

The concept of additionality is however, one of the many strengths of GNVQs in that it allows students to build a qualification which fits in with their interests and aspirations. In addition, many HE institutions may well require additions to the basic GNVQ for admission to some of their courses. You need to take this into account when planning your teaching.

Core skills

Core skills have been developed by NCVQ in six areas (Table 1.3). Since these units have been developed centrally the specification of the core skills does not differ between awarding bodies. Table 1.3 shows how the different levels of core skill units fit with the National Curriculum.

Table 1.3 *Core skill units*

Mandatory units	Additional units
1. Communication	4. Working with others
2. Application of Number	5. Improving own learning & performance
3. Application of Information Technology	6. Problem solving

Currently all students must achieve the three mandatory core skill units in **Communication, Application of Number** and **Application of Information Technology** at the appropriate level to achieve the award. For example, a student taking an Intermediate GNVQ must obtain all three mandatory core skill units at least at Level 2 in order to obtain the award. Students taking any GNVQ can, however, be awarded core skill units at a level higher than the award they are taking. For example, students taking the Advanced Science GNVQ may be working at Level 5 in the Application of Number and, providing they complete all the requirements for the unit, they can be awarded that unit at Level 5 as part of their Advanced GNVQ.

The other three core skill units are available but not necessary for the achievement of an award. Two of the units, **Personal Skills – Working with others** and **Personal Skills – Improving own learning and performance**, are assessed in the same way as the three mandatory core skill units and if the candidate is successful can be accredited by the awarding body and recorded on the GNVQ certificate. **Problem solving** is currently not accredited in this way but achievement in this area can be recorded on the student's National Record of Achievement. Higher Education and Employers will be looking for development in the these three additional core skill areas.

Developing and implementing strategies for teaching core skills has proved to be particularly tricky so Theme 2 is devoted to this subject.

> A major difference between GNVQs and other courses I have taught on is the idea of core skills. This is completely new to me. (GNVQ science teacher)

However, it is worth noting here that successful core skill delivery in current GNVQ centres nearly always involves a co-ordinated approach which includes both specialist teachers in the vocational area and core skill teachers working together as a team. As a subject specialist you cannot assume that someone else will be able to deliver core skills without reference to you: as a core skills teacher you cannot assume you can deliver core skills successfully in isolation from the vocational area being studied by the student.

KEY IDEA: Core skills should be developed and assessed as an integral part of the vocational programme.

1.4 INSIDE A GNVQ UNIT

To help you understand the terminology used to describe a GNVQ unit we will use a real example (Table 1.4). However, the notes will be equally applicable to a unit drawn from the GNVQ that you are working on so you can use that if you like. Do not worry at this stage about how you develop a scheme of work for your students from the unit. Just concentrate on trying to understand what the terminology means. The unit used here is one of the eight mandatory vocational units in the Advanced Health and Social Care GNVQ.

Any GNVQ unit consists of

- a unique **unit title** – in this case Interpersonal Interaction (Advanced)
- a unique **unit code** – this depends on the awarding body
- a number of **elements of achievement** – in this case there are three elements of achievement. Only one of these is given in full.

Each element of achievement consists of:

- the specification of an activity which the student has to achieve
- a number of **performance criteria**
- a **range statement**
- **evidence indicators** for vocational units.

The relationship between these components is shown in Figure 1.4.

Elements of achievement

These statements are the basic building blocks of a GNVQ. You need to interpret them within the framework of competence which

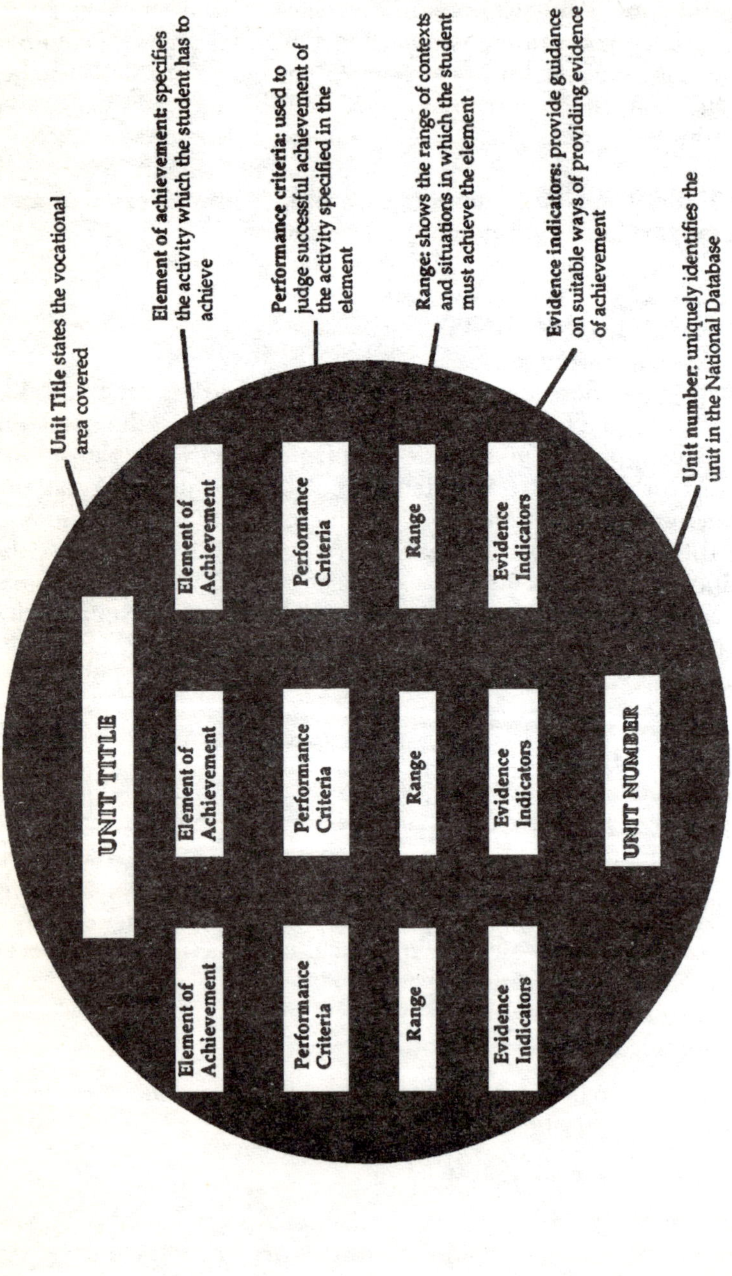

Figure 1.4 *The structure of a GNVQ unit.*

underpins GNVQ. To do this you need to understand at this stage something about how GNVQs are assessed. Understanding how GNVQs are assessed is fundamental to understanding how they work. Chapter 3 deals with assessment at length. For the moment you need to realise that GNVQs assess outcomes and are based on a competency model. This means that students have to show that they can do something in order to be assessed.

For example look at Element 2.2 in Table 1.4. To achieve this element students have got to demonstrate that they can 'Promote communication within groups'. This may involve students being introduced to ideas about, and the skills involved in, group communication through reading, simulations, videos and didactic teaching methods, but these activities alone are not sufficient to demonstrate competence and so pass this element. At the end of the day students have got to be able to demonstrate they can 'Promote communication within groups' by producing evidence of their competence in this area. This means that GNVQs are student-centred qualifications with the onus being placed on the student to:

> take a leading role in assessment by collecting and presenting evidence to make sure that they cover all the requirements of the elements ... (RSA (1993b) p17)

KEY IDEA: Elements of achievement set out the skills, knowledge and understanding which underpin performance. They represent activities which a student must achieve.

Performance criteria

Each element of achievement has a number of performance criteria which tell the student what they have to do in more detail to meet the requirements of the element. The student has to demonstrate an acceptable level of performance in each of the performance criteria to pass the element. This means that all performance criteria must be met for the award of a unit and that means that in your planning you must ensure that you provide your students with opportunities to meet them.

Notice:

- Performance criteria are specified as processes: they are things which the student has to do rather than just be told about.
- Performance criteria are very much minimum statements of competence: they set out only the essential aspects of performance necessary to achieve the outcome.

Table 1.4 *A mandatory unit from the Advanced GNVQ in Health and Social Care*

Unit 2 Interpersonal Interaction (Advanced)

The unit consists of three elements:

2.1 Communicate with individuals
2.2 Promote communication within groups
2.3 Analyse clients' rights in interpersonal situations

Each of these elements has four performance criteria, giving a total of 12 performance criteria for the unit. We will examine Element 2.2.

Element 2.2 Promote communication within groups

Performance criteria:

1. the method of communication maintains group cohesion
2. communication techniques are used to convey effective supportive skills
3. the form of communication conveys positive value of others
4. factors which inhibit interpersonal interaction are explained and avoided

Range:
Method of communication: verbal; non verbal

Communication techniques: face to face; tone of voice, body language, oral signals (eg ums, ahs); reflection of own and others' behaviour; active listening and responding

Supportive skills: conveying warmth, conveying understanding, conveying sincerity

Factors: distractions, dominating, manipulating, blocking others' contributions; culturally dependent behaviour

Positive value of others: respect for others, personal preference, choice, independence

Evidence indicators:

A project based on practical group communication work with peers and an investigation of group communication in a health or social care context.

Evidence should demonstrate understanding of the implications of the range dimensions in relation to the element. The unit test will confirm the candidate's coverage of range.

The specification of the performance criteria:

- Means the students should know exactly what they have to do to demonstrate their competence in a particular element.
- Allows you to explain to students why they have not achieved a particular element and what else they need to do in order to achieve the element.
- Makes the assessment process open, co-operative and student centred.

KEY IDEA: Performance criteria are used to judge whether the evidence presented by the student is sufficient to meet the requirements of an element of achievement.

Range

For each element, a range is identified which indicates the depth and extent of coverage that the student has to demonstrate to meet the requirements of the element. The range effectively places clear limits around the areas of knowledge which the student has to demonstrate achievement in. The range can also specify the contexts in which the student should demonstrate their competence. Each student must provide evidence (see below) that they have covered the complete range for each element of achievement.

A common mistake for teachers new to GNVQ is to interpret the range statements as though they were like a traditional teaching syllabus. They certainly set out what the students need to understand in order to pass a particular element but they also specify the contexts and ways in which students need to demonstrate their competence.

KEY IDEA: Range statements indicate how the student must demonstrate the element and the underpinning knowledge required for the element.

Evidence indicators

These indicate the type of evidence the student has to produce in order to demonstrate that the performance criteria and range have been covered. In the case of the unit shown in Table 1.4, the student has to present a project based around practical group communication. Such a project could contain evidence of background reading relating to the range and video material which analyses interactions between fellow students in terms of theory about group communication.

Evidence

The notion of evidence and its generation by students to demonstrate their competence is central to GNVQs. Evidence may include written reports, letters, sets of notes, tapes, videos and artefacts. These may be based on assignments, case studies and work based activities which are assembled to form a portfolio of evidence. In addition the portfolio of evidence may contain supplementary evidence that the student has covered all of the range statements. This may take the form of internal or external tests, notes or ephemeral evidence, e.g. oral presentations. This latter category could also include conversations between tutor and students which show that they have understood a particular idea but which is not obvious from, say, a written assignment. You should record details of such conversations in note form on the student's work. It is the portfolio of evidence which is submitted by a candidate to support their claim for certification and is therefore a record of the student's achievements.

The final statement at the end of the element of achievement in Table 1.4 also requires some explanation. Each mandatory unit has associated with it an externally set unit test which will confirm whether a student has developed the knowledge and understanding suggested in the range. However, in their portfolio of evidence students have got to go a little further than this: they have to show an understanding of how all the things specified in the range come together to enable them to show their competence in a particular element. The demonstration of this synthetic, evaluative thinking lies at the heart of the **grading criteria** for GNVQ which are discussed further in Chapter 3.

1.5 ROLES AND RESPONSIBILITIES

One of the other bewildering things about GNVQs for newcomers is the wide range of people with strange titles who are involved. Table 1.5 sets out some key titles and the responsibilities these people or groups have. The major notion that needs to be taken on board here is that GNVQs are best delivered by a team of people called the course team, who are responsible for devising the learning programme. Such a team will, ideally, consist of vocational

experts and core skills specialists. One or more m
course team will have been trained as assessors
passed the NVQ units D32 and D33. These are the p
officially assess students' work. They are monitored
verifier who has had further training and passed
units. Overall monitoring of the programme in a c...ge is the responsibility of an external verifier who is appointed by the awarding body.

Table 1.5 *Roles and responsibilities in running a GNVQ course. These are some terms you will meet later in this book*

Title	**Function**
Course team	Plans the learning and assessment programme; plans induction programme; arranges tutorial support; ensures learning support systems are in place and are staffed; timetables and allocates responsibilities to each member of the team
Teacher	Monitors student progress on assignments; provides day to day guidance; plans learning activities with students; teaches through formal inputs and in workshops; enables students to identify their learning needs and to access learning support systems
Personal tutor	Monitors long-term progress of student through regular review meetings; conducts initial assessments with student during induction; identifies appropriate learning activities with students and guides them to learning support services; ensures student has access to learning support, e.g. workshops
Course tutor	Manages and teaches on a course; is sometimes the personal tutor as well
Assessor	Teacher who has passed the NVQ unit D33 and possibly D32 so qualifying them to assess GNVQ
Internal verifier	A teacher from outside the course team who has passed the additional NVQ unit D34. Responsible for moderating assessments made by assessors
External verifier	A person appointed from outside the institution by the awarding body to oversee the running of GNVQ courses in a school or college

ΓHINKING ABOUT TEACHING GNVQs

By now you are probably thinking 'How do I teach this?'. Answering that question forms the basis of the next chapter but there is a key principle worth stating here.

KEY IDEA: A GNVQ unit is an assessment framework, not a teaching syllabus. A GNVQ unit is not a unit of learning: it is a unit of assessment.

This opens up exciting possibilities for you as a teacher of GNVQs and for your students. Make no mistake, GNVQs need teaching but you will find yourself having to use a wide range of teaching methodologies some of which may not be all that familiar to you. In addition, the actual content of the teaching syllabus is not being specified in any detail: you have to decide therefore what opportunities you are going to give your students to produce the evidence they need for their portfolios. What this might involve is well summed up in the following quote which, whilst it is talking specifically about Business GNVQ, is applicable to all GNVQ teaching and learning:

> In business innovating and problem solving are essential skills. Creative and analytical thinking is developed in GNVQs through investigating, making and justifying proposals for improvements, predicting and planning. Centres and candidates are encouraged to use the unit specifications as an assessment framework and to be imaginative in their learning programmes, engaging in such activities as business enterprise, work experience, work shadowing and business education partnerships. These activities should directly assist the candidate in producing evidence. For example a work experience placement could offer opportunities for customer service at GNVQ2 and for investigating systems at GNVQ3. A Young Enterprise programme could produce evidence towards most of the units at both levels 2 and 3. (RSA (1993a) p4)

Putting all of these into practice may seem a daunting prospect but it is an exciting one. Do not be afraid to cut your units up and rearrange them so that you can produce meaningful learning activities for your students. The reward is, of course, in seeing young people who may have been poorly served by the education system in the past succeeding and growing in self-confidence.

Go for it – but be prepared for a lot of hard work and the need for commitment from staff which will then be rewarded by the attitude and quality of work your students will demonstrate. (Department of Employment (1993) p2)

Chapter 2

Getting Started with Teaching GNVQs

Teaching practically anything involves operating within a set of constraints. Some of these will be external to an institution, e.g. exam syllabuses, modes of assessment and others internal to it – amount of teaching time, access to facilities like computers, staffing and so on. Effective teaching depends, in part at least, on recognising and taking account of these constraints when planning a learning programme. The first steps in getting to grips with GNVQ must, therefore, involve working out the constraints it imposes on you in terms of both what you teach and how you teach it. This is not an easy task since there are many factors you have to take into account. To simplify the task, and so get you started, this first section of the book only considers those constraints imposed by the mandatory vocational units: what the units mean and how they are assessed. Another set of constraints, core skills, will be introduced in the second section of the book, and the final set, to do with management of student learning, forms the final section.

However, what I cannot do is simply provide you with a recipe of how to teach GNVQ. That would be extremely foolhardy and arrogant because GNVQ units are, essentially, units of assessment and not units of learning. Therefore, how GNVQs are actually delivered is, within certain constraints, entirely up to each individual centre. This point is even emphasised in the literature produced by the awarding bodies:

> Learning programmes are not prescribed by City and Guilds. Centres are free to design their own and are encouraged to draw as widely as possible on available resources within and outside the institution. (City and Guilds (1993) p21)

Educational institutions, be they schools or colleges, differ in so many ways that a simple, unique prescription of how to teach GNVQ would apply to few if any. You will have, for example, different physical resources, timetabling arrangements, links with industry and business and differences in your own expertise compared with other institutions. Combining all of these factors together means that GNVQ programmes in different institutions look quite different. You can certainly learn from how current GNVQ programmes are running; you can probably copy bits in the first instance; but to try and copy the whole programme from one institution to another would probably be disastrous. It is much better for you to work through how a GNVQ course can best be run in your institution. In that way you will understand what you have to teach and how you can best do this in your institution. In the first instance this involves working out the external constraints imposed by the GNVQ model of the curriculum.

2.1 PRELIMINARY THINKING

Reading the GNVQ units and making sense of them is the first hurdle you have to overcome. GNVQ units do not look like conventional subject syllabuses nor do they look like traditional BTEC units, for example. The following reaction is not uncommon:

> I was just given the units and basically told to get on with it. When I opened the first unit my reaction was one of shock. I had never seen anything like this, the jargon, and I couldn't find anything which told me what I had to teach. Where was the content? How could students take and pass the tests if I didn't know what I had to teach them? (Intermediate manufacturing GNVQ teacher)

This response, from an experienced teacher, essentially arises from confusion about what the extensive GNVQ documentation is actually saying. (GNVQ is one of the most extensively documented courses around!) Understandably some teachers have tried to interpret the GNVQ units as though they were a traditional teaching syllabus and have constructed their teaching programmes on this premise:

> I used the range which looked a bit like a syllabus to get started. After about a month when I was doing the first assessment I realised something was wrong though. The kids all had beautiful notes which I had given them but they did not meet any of the performance criteria of the unit I was teaching. I had done all the work they had done little and so could not provide the evidence needed. I realised then I needed to think about this more. (Intermediate GNVQ teacher – Health & Social Care)

Neither of these reactions is intended to put you off, though you may be reassured to find that you are not alone if you too are wondering what the units are telling you to do. Usually attendance at the training sessions run by one of the awarding bodies sort out these early misconceptions. (It is worth going to these training sessions in pairs so that you can discuss and clarify understandings about what you should be doing.) However what both these comments do suggest is that you have got to work out what you have to teach.

GNVQs are new, unique qualifications and they are specified in quite different ways to, say, GCSE or A level. Furthermore, the units are presented in quite a complex form, using unfamiliar language and concepts. This Chapter is designed to help you understand what the GNVQ units are actually saying and help you begin to answer two key questions which emerge from the teacher comments quoted above:

What should I teach?
How should I teach it?

To answer these two questions you need, initially, two documents: a copy of the mandatory vocational units that you will be teaching and a copy of the **test specification** which goes with each of these units.

KEY IDEA: What students have to learn to pass a GNVQ is worked out using the unit and test specifications.

2.2 READING THE ELEMENTS

The first step in understanding the **mandatory vocational units** is realising what the **elements of achievement** (abbreviated to elements) and their associated **performance criteria** are saying. Below are the first elements from the first mandatory vocational unit for five **Advanced GNVQs.** (If you do not understand the terms in bold above, you need to read the first chapter!)

- Explore the application of light and colour in two-dimensional work
  (Art and Design Advanced GNVQ: UNIT 1 Two Dimensional Visual Language)
- Explain the purposes and products of business
  (Business Advanced GNVQ: UNIT 1 Business in the Economy)

- Investigate attitudes and other social influences on behaviour (Health and Social Care Advanced GNVQ: UNIT 1 Access, Equal Opportunities and Client Rights)
- Describe the scale and contexts of the leisure and tourism industry
  (Leisure and Tourism Advanced GNVQ : UNIT 1 Investigating the Leisure and Tourism Industry)
- Prepare product specifications
  (Manufacturing Advanced GNVQ: UNIT 1 Design Specification)

I could have chosen any other elements from any other GNVQ: they would all have a similar format to these. Elements are the fundamental building blocks of a GNVQ and it is from these that you have to begin to plan your teaching. The problem is understanding what they mean and so working out what your students have to learn.

A question of competence

To really get to grips with GNVQ, and what the unit specifications mean, requires an understanding of three related concepts: **standards, competence** and **learning outcomes**. Understanding these terms will help greatly in the planning of appropriate learning activities for your students.

The historical development of GNVQ requires another book to do it justice. Suffice to say here that the terminology of standards, competence and learning outcomes began to develop in a coherent way in the early 1980s as a result of concern in the Department of Employment about low levels of skill in the British work-force compared with our major competitors. This thinking, especially that of Gilbert Jessup, led to the development of standards-based qualifications, the most familiar of which is now National Vocational Qualifications (NVQs). It is from this thinking that GNVQs and the way they are specified in terms of elements of achievement and performance criteria evolved.

The key difference between this 'new' thinking and that associated with more traditional courses, like A level or BTEC National Diplomas, was a shift from an education system largely defined in terms of its inputs to one defined by its outputs. Some definitions will help here:

Inputs = syllabuses, the course, training programmes, i.e. specifications of the learning opportunities provided.

Outputs = the 'standards' which need to be achieved by the end of a programme of learning.

'Standards' = 'a clear specification of the performance required of an individual including the level or standard of performance ... this is set out in a statement of competence.' (Bees and Swords (1990) p18)

GNVQs are standards-based qualifications. The standards are expressed in the form of statements which specify what the student has to achieve at the end of a programme of learning to gain the award. These statements in GNVQ are the elements of achievement. Students have to accumulate evidence, in the form of a **portfolio of work**, which shows they have achieved each of the elements within a GNVQ programme. Whether the evidence they produce meets the required standard for each element is judged or assessed using the performance criteria associated with each element. So it is the joint specification of

- elements of achievement
- performance criteria

which set the standard that the student has to reach and that provide the goals or learning outcomes for the teaching and learning programme.

KEY IDEA: Simply engaging in a learning activity which relates to an element of achievement is not sufficent to pass the element. Students must produce evidence which meets the requirement of each of the performance criteria associated with the element. It is the outcome that matters.

2.3 IMPLICATIONS FOR TEACHING

This notion of competent performance and the way the elements of achievement are specified immediately identifies a major constraint affecting the way you teach GNVQ. By their nature GNVQs force teaching to be more student-centred and more active than might be the case with, say, an A level course. To pass a GNVQ students must generate evidence of achievement based on their own work, course work if you like, usually set by the teacher in the form of an **assignment**. As you will see later, other sources of evidence can also be used by students to demonstrate achievement on GNVQs but it is the assignment work which will form the bulk of a student's portfolio of evidence. You will come across examples of assignments later.

KEY IDEA: The dominant mode of teaching and learning on GNVQ courses needs to be through student-centred assignments.

So do I need to teach anything?

It is one of the great myths of the student-centred, active learning approaches implied by the GNVQ model that teachers, in some sense, do not have to teach. This is because teaching is equated with just standing at the front of a class and talking and that such an activity is not consistent with active student-centred approaches. Both of these ideas are wrong. A good lecture can be a very active learning experience for a student and teaching involves far more than just lecturing.

> I certainly spend less time lecturing on this course. But that means I really think about what I'm going to say and my lectures are better ... more enjoyable for me and the student. (GNVQ Business teacher)

It is worth stressing at this stage, therefore, that GNVQs do need teaching and teachers are at the centre of devising good GNVQ programmes. Teachers organise the learning programme, explain GNVQ to their students and devise the learning experiences which will enable those students to be successful. GNVQ students will require a wide range of different experiences and engage in a wider range of activities (see Table 2.1) to be successful, probably more than they would encounter on say an A level or a GCSE course, and this does have implications for the way you teach GNVQ. But you should not think that you have got to reinvent the wheel and teach in radically different ways from the way you do now. Much of your current practice will be appropriate to GNVQ but you may have to add other elements or shift the emphasis a bit.

But what do I have to teach?

This question still remains unaswered but what this section does suggest is that it is the wrong question. In a standards-based system like GNVQ the question needs to be rephrased to:

What does this student need to learn about and do in order to achieve that particular element?

Table 2.1 *The following list illustrates the variety of activities which GNVQ students could engage in to generate the evidence needed to demonstrate their achievement (From:* Assessing Core Skills, *NCVQ, 1994)*

Observing	Drawing	Modelling	Writing
Listening	Role play	Reading	Talking
Planning	Measuring	Calculating	Composing
Wordprocessing	Evaluating	Physical activity	Researching
Assessing	Questioning	Recalling	Reviewing
Designing	Singing	Map reading	Experimenting
Collecting	Performing	Problem solving	Selecting
Illustrating	Translating	Investigating	Discussing
Watching	Computing	Making	Answering
Copying	Asking	Interviewing	Surveying

Within the context of a GNVQ course, then, the role of the teacher can best be defined as providing opportunities for students which will enable them to produce the evidence needed to satisfy the standard specified by the elements and associated performance criteria. Remember, to be awarded a GNVQ unit a student has to pass every single element, which means meeting all the performance criteria for each element. You might like to compare this with what a student has to do to achieve an A level pass. A few moments reflection will help you realise that GNVQs are not easy qualifications to obtain and your students will have to work hard and be highly motivated if they are going to succeed. However, GNVQ students do know exactly what they have to do in order to be successful: it is written down. The problem is that they, like you, have to understand and interpret the available information.

The GNVQ teacher's problem can now be stated something like this:

What have I got to teach this class so that they can satisfy the performance criteria of this particular element?

Put another way we can ask:

What knowledge and skills do these students need to develop in order to satisfy the performance criteria of this particular element? How best can I, as the teacher, ensure that the students acquire this knowledge and develop these skills?

Implicit in this question is the idea that underpinning the generating of evidence of achievement are essential knowledge and skills. We can illustrate this idea in a rather trite way by considering driving a car. We want drivers to be competent and a driving test assesses the level of your competence by making sure you can drive a car safely. For you to be able to do that you have been taught the skills of driving plus, for example, knowledge about the highway code. What is important though is that you can drive the car safely and competently, i.e. the emphasis is placed on successful performance rather than the underpinning knowledge and skills. These are tested by showing you can actually do something to an acceptable level which is clearly specified. This is the idea behind GNVQ.

We can take this simple analogy a little further. Imagine three drivers. One has been driving a car around a farm and already has the skills of changing gear, using the brakes and accelerator. After just one or two lessons this individual is ready to take and pass the test. The second individual has never driven a car before but learns the skills rapidly and after 15 lessons is ready to take and pass the test. The third individual fails the test the first time. The examiner identifies areas which need further work; the driving instructor helps the learner to further develop these skills. The test is retaken and passed.

GNVQs are like this too. Individuals will develop underpinning skills and knowledge at different rates and in different ways. Accordingly they will demonstrate achievement in different ways and at different times. Some students will progress faster than others. Some may not succeed the first time so they will need to be given extra opportunities to show they have satisified the performance criteria. Others may be able to satisfy the performance criteria very quickly with remarkably little learning because they already have the necessary skills and knowledge. Furthermore, at the end of the day what matters is the evidence that students produce, not how it is produced. This means that students could produce evidence of achievement from work experience, their part-time jobs, community work or their hobbies. GNVQ will therefore require teachers to pay greater attention to the individual learning needs of their students. This suggests that GNVQ teaching will, therefore, involve:

- the extensive use of assignments on which students work independently of the teacher
- careful management of students learning
- lots of individual tutorial work in which students plans and progress are discussed.

2.4 UNDERPINNING KNOWLEDGE AND UNDERSTANDING

To satisfy the performance criteria and so pass an element means that students need to acquire knowledge and understanding. Deciding what that knowledge and understanding is for each element will help you to begin to decide what to teach, how and when. You do have to take other design features of GNVQ into account in devising programmes of learning as well, for example core skill development, but in coming to grips with GNVQ it is better at this stage to ignore these.

The next problem is therefore to decide what the knowledge, understanding and skills are that students need to pass an element. This is not immediately obvious from looking at the unit specification. So whilst the NCVQ confidently and correctly maintains that 'GNVQ units set out in some detail the outcomes that students must achieve' (NCVQ (1993a) p9), the content the students need to cover is not immediately obvious. Two other aspects of GNVQ will help in the search for the underpinning knowledge and skills which are essential to enable the student to:

- produce the evidence necessary to meet the performance criteria associated with each element
- pass the external test associated with each mandatory vocational unit.

These are the **range statements** associated with each element of achievement and another set of documents called the **test specifications**. How these can be used will be exemplified with a case study using one element from a mandatory vocational Health and Social Care unit as an example, but the general principles of working would be the same for all GNVQs.

Range statements

GNVQs are not designed to be narrow qualifications. Consequently students produce evidence which meets the performance criteria for each element not just in one but in a range of contexts. This range of contexts is set out in the range statements. For example consider Unit 4 of the Intermediate Health and Social Care GNVQ: Health and Social Care Services. This unit has three elements concerned with the structure, access to and clients rights within health and care services. Element 4.1 is set out in Table 2.2.

Table 2.2 *One element from the Intermediate Health and Social Care unit, Health and Social Care Services*

Element 4.1 Identify the structure of health and care services

Performance Criteria
1. the overall organisation of health and care services is described
2. the general purpose of different services is described
3. the relationship of key services to each other is explained

Range:
Organisation of health and care services: DSS; Department of Health; NHS; Health authorities, voluntary and private; service structures in Northern Ireland

Key services: hospitals; dentists' and doctors' surgeries; community and residential services for children, disabled people and elders.

Evidence indicators:
A project to identify and describe the structure of services.

Evidence should demonstrate understanding of the implications of the range dimensions in relation to the element. The unit test will confirm the candidate's coverage of range.

To pass this element students have to produce evidence, in the form of a project (look at the evidence indicator at the end of the specification), which identifies and describes the structure of health services. Just producing such a project is not, in itself, sufficient: the student's evidence must meet the three performance criteria. So the project has to describe the overall organisation of health and care services, the general purpose of the different services and the relationship between the key services. But which services? This is where the range comes in. This identifies the services which the students needs to know about. So teaching this element will involve organising learning activities which enable the students to produce a project about the organisations and services listed in the range which meet the performance criteria for the element.

KEY IDEA: Student's portfolios of work must contain evidence that they have met the performance criteria associated with a particular element and that they have covered the range associated with the element.

If you look through the range statements associated with just one of the mandatory units you are going to teach or look at the specification for the unit being considered here (Table 2.3) you will immediately realise that GNVQ students have to learn a lot.

> My immediate concern, having understood what the units were telling me, was how much I had to cover. (GNVQ Business teacher)

The implications of this for teaching will be discussed in the next section.

Test specifications

These are separate sets of documents, one document for each GNVQ. The guidelines for the test specifications have been agreed between all examining bodies, so, like the mandatory unit specifications, the test specifications are the same for all awarding bodies. Inside the test specification documents you will find:

- a guide to the principles of external tests and their design
- categories of knowledge included in and design of the test specifications themselves
- example test questions which will give you some idea about the level of knowledge and depth of understanding required as well as indicating the range of question formats to be used. Note that these need to be used cautiously as the tests were being revised at the time of writing
- detailed test specifications which set out further details of the knowledge and understanding that will be assessed using the external tests on a unit by unit basis.

The external tests are essentially designed to ensure that students have fully covered the essential knowledge underpinning a particular unit: they assess whether students have understood the knowledge and skills underpinning the performance criteria and that they have covered the complete range as specified in the range statements. The test specifications are, therefore, valuable sources of additional information about what your students need to have learnt to pass the unit test and so they give additional information as to the knowledge they need to have acquired to meet the performance criteria set out in the unit specifications. However, they do not replace the unit specifications: they supplement them and both documents should be read together. Indeed you may find it useful to take pair of scissors to photocopies of both documents and do a cut and paste job to produce a working document which contains both sets of information.

Table 2.3 *Unit 4 Health and Social Care Services (Intermediate)*

Element 4.1: Identify the structure of health and care services	**Element 4.2: Examine access to health and care services**	**Element 4.3: Identify client rights in health and care services**
Performance criteria: 1. the overall organisation of health and care services is described 2. the general purpose of different services is described 3. the relationship of key services to each other is explained	**Performance criteria:** 1. the needs of different client groups within the community are described 2. the role of different groups of health and care workers is identified 3. key sources of information on health and care services are identified 4. means of access/referral to health and care services in the community are explained in relation to client needs	**Performance criteria:** 1. the importance of maintaining client rights is explained 2. methods for encouraging independence and choice for clients are identified 3. the need to maintain confidentiality of information about clients is explained 4. legislation which promotes freedom from discrimination is identified
Range: **Organisation of health and care services:** DSS; Dept of Health; NHS; Health authorities; local authorities, voluntary and private; service structures in Northern Ireland **Key Services:** hospitals; dentists' and doctors' surgeries; community and residential services for children, disabled people and elders	**Range:** **Needs of different client groups:** physical; social; emotional; cultural; educational **Key sources of information:** DSS; Citizens Advice Bureau; Post Office; GP and dentist reception; health clinics; libraries **Health and care workers:** medical and nursing staff; health support workers; paramedical staff; social workers; social care staff; staff in early education; role of staff within statutory, voluntary and private services **Client groups:** children; adolescents; disabled people; elders	**Range:** **Legislation:** race equality; gender equality; disability equality **Clients:** any people using health and care services **Client rights:** freedom from discrimination; dignity; independence; choice; confidentiality; health and safety **Methods:** designed into service delivery; within conversations with clients
Evidence Indicators: A project to identify and describe structure of services	**Evidence indicators:** A project which explains access to health and care services in relation to one client group	**Evidence indicators:** A project to identify the rights of clients in relation to any one health or care service

However, the test specifications are incomplete sources of information since:

- test specifications are only available for those mandatory vocational units which are assessed with an external test and they do not cover optional or core skill units since these are not assessed externally.
- some elements in some GNVQs require a local study, and setting a national external test to assess local detail is clearly impossible. However, where general principles and understanding can be drawn from such studies these are tested.

This means that some performance criteria and occasionally a complete element are not included in the test specifications.

Given these two riders the test specifications are useful since:

- they do identify the knowledge and understanding in mandatory units which will be assessed and which therefore the students have to learn
- they allocate a proportion of marks to that knowledge and understanding.

However, do not think you are going to find a conventional A level or GCSE syllabus. Associated with the test specifications is another set of jargon that you have to learn. In particular you need to understand the meaning of the word **focus**. If you open your test specification for the GNVQ that you are going to teach you will find after the initial preamble detailed test specifications. These have the form shown in Table 2.4.

The test specification for each unit is divided up into a series of focuses. The idea here is that '... focuses [...] have concise headings indicating the areas of knowledge and understanding that they cover'. (Royal Society of Arts (1993c) p3). The unit chosen here, Unit 4 of the Intermediate GNVQ in Health and Social Care has five such focuses. Under each focus there is a set of references to the elements and performance criteria (abbreviated to PC) and the part of the range statements which this particular focus covers. The unit specification for this unit is set out in Table 2.4 so you can compare the two. Finally there is a list of **knowledge statements** and the number of marks which will be allocated to that focus in the external test which might give you some idea of the relative importance of the different focuses.

Notice that four of the focuses (2, 3, 4, 5) refer to only some of the performance criteria from one element of the test specification whilst one focus, 1, refers to 2 elements. This is a common pattern

Table 2.4 *Test specifications for Unit 4: Health and Social Care Services – (Intermediate)*

Focus 1: Services and Personnel

References

Element 4.1, PC 1, 2, 3
Range: Organisation of health and care services, Key services

Knowledge

(a) Describe the organisation of key health and care services
(b) Identify the general purpose of different services
(c) Compare the relationships between key services

Marks **10**

Focus 2: Personnel and Sources of Information

References

Element 4.2, PC 2, 3
Range: Health and care workers, Key sources of information

Knowledge

(a) Identify the roles of different health and care workers
(b) Identify key sources of information on health and care services

Marks **7**

Focus 3: Client Needs

References

Element 4.2, PC 1, 4
Range: Needs of different client groups, Client groups

Knowledge

(a) Identify the needs of different client groups within the community
(b) Select the means of access/referral to health and care services in the community in relation to client needs

Marks **10**

Focus 4: Client Rights

References

Element 4.3, PC 1, 2, 3
Range: Clients rights, Methods

Knowledge

(a) Explain the importance of maintaining client rights
(b) Identify methods of encouraging independence and choice for clients
(c) Identify reasons why confidentiality of information about clients is maintained

Marks **7**

Focus 5: Legislation

References

Element 4.3, PC 4
Range: Legislation; Client rights

Knowledge

(a) Identify legislation which promotes freedom from discrimination

Marks **3**

Total marks **37**

across all the unit test specifications, i.e. 'knowledge statements in a focus may be limited to performance criteria from a single element but some may cross elements in a single unit'. Each focus also relates to only a limited part of the range. This format serves to re-emphasise that the GNVQ units specify an approach to assessment not an approach to teaching. In other words in terms of teaching it might make little sense to teach a unit element by element as though you could treat these separately, since the test specifications suggest the knowledge required cuts across the elements or the same body of knowledge may be required in two different elements. Indeed underpinning knowledge in practice actually involves jumps across the unit boundaries themselves which may result in some poorly planned teaching which duplicates what has gone before.

> Time and again during the course of the year my students have told me they had already covered something I was trying to teach them. At first I put this down to students always saying that sort of thing. Then it dawned on me that the knowledge requirements were duplicated and some of my colleagues were teaching things I thought I was supposed to be teaching. This was just bad planning. (Intermediate Health & Social Care teacher)

The implications of this are, I think, clear. Before you start teaching GNVQ you must have a complete overview of the knowledge and understanding requirements which underpin the whole of the qualification. This is a massive mapping exercise but one which is worth doing since it will enable you to provide a logical structure to the course you are going to teach. This will help to ensure that both you and your students know what is happening and will facilitate the recording of progress.

The knowledge statements themselves attempt to distinguish between three categories of knowledge:

- Descriptions and definitions, e.g. Describe the organisation of key health and care services (Focus 1, Table 2.4)
- Comparisons and relationships between some of the range statements that need to be understood, e.g. Compare the relationships between key services (Focus 1, Table 2.4)
- Analytical or evaluative skills and understanding that are expected, e.g. Select the means of access/referral to health and care services in the community in relation to client needs (Focus 3, Table 2.4).

There is therefore an increased complexity in the knowledge and understanding required as you go down the list and this is reflected in the fact that Advanced GNVQs will have a greater number of questions testing knowledge categories 2 and 3 than Intermediate. This suggests a difference in emphasis in teaching between Advanced and Intermediate with more emphasis being placed upon higher order understanding and skills being developed in Advanced GNVQs. This should be reflected in the teaching approaches used with and the demands made of Intermediate and Advanced candidates.

At the time of writing, test specifications were not available for Foundation GNVQs but extrapolation would suggest that tests for mandatory units at Foundation level will concentrate more on category 1 than category 3 knowledge. Foundation GNVQ students should, though, be given the opportunity to develop and practise the skills need for dealing with knowledge and understanding in category 3 since this will be essential for successful progression, either on to another educational course or for training in the workplace within the NVQ framework.

So what do they need to know?

The unit specifications and the range represent, at the moment, the two major sources of information available to you about the content you have to cover. Ideally you would also like access to a bank of test questions and completed assignments since this would give you an even better idea of what you have to cover and, more importantly, the level. These will become available through time and, combined with your own growing confidence and experience of GNVQ, will mean that you will know what you have to teach and at what level. This is not a criticism of GNVQ: it is true of all new qualifications when they are introduced. I can remember going through exactly the same problems with GCSE for example. It just takes time.

However, from the information available in the unit and test specification I know that students have to learn about the following to pass element 4.1 from this health and social care unit.

The structure and organisation of the following:

- Department of Social Security
- Department of Health
- National Health Service
- Local Health Authorities

- Local Authority services
- voluntary and private services
- service structures in Northern Ireland.

Students also need to understand how these relate to each other and how they control and manage key services like:

- hospitals
- dentists' and doctors' surgeries
- various community and residential services, e.g. children's homes and nursing homes.

For each of these services students need to have a general idea of what each service does and again how they relate to each other. This suggests therefore that what students should be building up is some sort of organisational diagram which indicates not only what these key services do but how they relate to each other. The big problem now is how much detail to go into. With an established exam system you could rely on textbooks and old exam papers to help you answer this. But GNVQ is still too young for either of these to be much help. You have, therefore, to learn this through experience. In the first instance it is probably better to go into more depth than you think is needed. Remembering that Intermediate is roughly equivalent to GCSE can also be useful.

The next step is to look at how this content relates to the content underpinning the other elements in the unit and then the extent to which similar content underpins other units. This may also include optional units. For example, one advanced science GNVQ course team had identified an optional unit in microbiology as providing useful underpinning knowledge for the mandatory science vocational unit concerned with making materials using living systems. Consequently they had combined these two units and taught them together. The important message here is do not think the units have to be a strait-jacket. At the end of the day it is up to you how you design your learning programme. Different approaches to this will be discussed in Chapter 4.

2.5 FURTHER IMPLICATIONS FOR TEACHING

A further set of constraints implicit in the vocational mandatory unit specifications can now be identified. The most important of these is concerned with time.

Fitting it all in

To obtain a GNVQ will require most students to learn and understand a lot of content. The temptation is to teach that content in a highly didactic manner, through lectures, for example. Let me reiterate, there is nothing wrong with a good lecture as a teaching methodology. However, if you use up all your contact time with the students in this way there will be little time left to support them in their work of generating the evidence needed to meet the performance criteria. Clearly a careful balancing act is needed, part of which must involve the need to get students to do more for themselves. This point is emphasised by the NCVQ:

> The responsibility that students take for their own learning and assessment is an important feature of GNVQ courses. It is made possible by ensuring that students clearly understand what they are expected to demonstrate to meet the requirements of the qualification. (NCVQ (1993a) p10)

This suggests that GNVQ teachers need to resist the temptation to do everything for the student: to give them all the notes. How might that work in practice? How do you enable young people to become more active learners and take responsibility when they may well be used to being highly passive learners? How do you overcome that feeling of 'Can I trust these students to complete this work, to the correct standard and on time?' This last question is really important since it suggests that part of the challenge of fitting it all in lies in examining your own views about teaching and your views about students. Part of the *raison d'être* of GNVQ is to enable students to develop the skills needed to complete work, to the correct standard and on time. Indeed they cannot pass the award, certainly at the higher grades, without being able to do this. The problem is that students need to be taught how to do it and that teaching needs to occur early on in the course. One of the issues to be considered when devising learning programmes then is the management of student learning and this will be reviewed in detail in section 3 of this book.

KEY IDEA: To pass the award GNVQ students must develop the skills needed to work independently of the teacher.

The need to collaborate

The large content that needs to be covered combined with the need to develop students' learning skills means that GNVQs have to be delivered in a tightly planned and highly organised way. This involves intense collaboration between both you and your students and between you and the other teachers – the course team – teaching on the course. Simply delegating responsibility to someone for teaching a unit and then telling them to get on with it in a vacuum is not likely to produce the results needed. There is a need for constant discussion to:

- clarify the meaning of the units
- plan the learning programme and write assignments
- monitor students' progress
- identify problems with the course structure
- review and modify the learning programme.

Developing a GNVQ course which works well is likely to take time and you will not get it perfect the first time. That is not a cause for despair but simply a realisation of the fact that learning to teach GNVQ is a complex process. It is going to take time for you to build up the necessary experience.

KEY IDEA: Successful GNVQ courses are underpinned by highly integrated course teams which meet regularly to discuss, plan and review the course.

Chapter 3

Assessing GNVQs

The nature of the GNVQ assessment process provides an important set of constraints on the way in which you teach GNVQ and you must take these into account at the course planning stage. In particular the processes and procedures of GNVQ assessment, combined with the underlying philosophy of GNVQ which emphasises students demonstrating what they can do, provides an additional rationale for teaching primarily through assignments rather than through more formal, didactic methods.

Assessment can be seen as the process which lies at the heart of teaching and learning on GNVQ courses. Thus NCVQ comments in several of its publications that: 'Assessment is seen as an integral part of learning during GNVQ programmes', whilst the awarding bodies, in the advice they provide to centres, also emphasise the centrality of assessment to GNVQ programmes. However, much of this advice is about what teachers and students have to do, with very little on how to do it. This has left many teachers in the early stages of the development of GNVQ in a real quandary. Whilst many support the approaches and methodology of GNVQ the complexity of the assessment arrangements has left many confused and unsure. For example one experienced vocational education teacher commented:

> When I see my students working and the motivation that the assignment approach generates I am full of enthusiasm for GNVQ. When it comes to marking assignments my enthusiasm rapidly wanes. It takes so long and I find interpreting the performance criteria in relation to real work being produced by students very difficult. Often the students have to take their work away to do a bit more in order to achieve a particular element and they can find that discouraging. Grading work has proven to be a nightmare.

This comment needs to be interpreted cautiously. There is nothing inherently mysterious about assessing GNVQs but they are young qualifications and there is not yet the body of expertise built up within the teaching profession nor the amount of exemplar material needed to help teachers make consistent judgements about students' work. However, the same was also true when GCSE was being introduced and that has turned out to be a great success.

KEY IDEA: New methods of assessment, especially the changing roles of teachers and students in the assessment process, inevitably cause uncertainty and confusion.

To a certain extent, then, you will need to accept that you will have to learn how to assess GNVQs as you go on. There really is no magic formula. The purpose of this chapter is to help you along the way by trying to get behind the jargon of the assessment process so you know exactly what you have to do, and to begin to suggest some general strategies on how to do it.

Above all, though, the key to assessing GNVQs is good planning and a course team approach. It really helps a lot if you constantly talk with your colleagues about assessment so that you adopt common policies and evolve common understandings, so developing consistency in the assessment process. This learning process should also be supported by the assessment infrastructure of assessors and verifiers and the training which you, yourself, will need to undertake in order to become a GNVQ assessor. Indeed you have to pass two NVQ units, so you will get first hand experience of being on the receiving end of outcomes based assessment methods. This process is described well by Ros Ollin and Jenny Tucker (1994).

3.1 AN OVERVIEW OF GNVQ ASSESSMENT

This section gives an overview of the assessment system. Difficult areas are explored in more detail in later sections where a case study is used to exemplify what one group of teachers were doing and thinking as they set and assessed an assignment.

Types of assessment

Essentially there are four types of assessment which occur on GNVQ courses:

- Internal continuous assessment
- Internal testing by centres
- Externally set testing
- Grading

The first and last of these are dealt with in more detail later.

Testing

External tests are designed to provide confirmation of knowledge and understanding as identified in the range statements and test specification for each mandatory vocational unit. These tests are made available by the awarding bodies on a number of occasions during the year; they offer a facility for retesting; and they are externally marked.

This regime of testing at fixed points rather than on demand has led many centres to work on a unit by unit basis so that students generate the evidence needed to meet the performance criteria and cover the range for one or two units and then take the test(s). If they fail then they retake the test at the next testing point. You can however, tackle the mandatory units in any order since any test can be taken at any testing point. Some centres have found this approach too constricting however:

> We were advised to adopt a unit by unit approach by our external verifier but when we tried to do that we found the course to be bitty and unsatisfying. We realised that the units were only an assessment strategy and that we were free to decide how we wanted to teach them. So we went back to the thematic approach we were using with our old BTEC course. We are happier with that and the students have had no problems with the tests. (GNVQ Art & Design Teacher)

This was, however, a very experienced BTEC course team and, whilst you should not let the external tests put your teaching into a strait-jacket, you do need to ensure that you do not get a log-jam of tests. It is much better for GNVQ students if the tests are spread out through the year and this must be a key factor which you take into account when planning the course.

KEY IDEA: Plan your course to spread the testing load evenly through it.

Currently the tests take the form of multiple choice items but concern expressed about the tests in the spring of 1994 led to more work being done on them in the summer as this book was being written. Consequently, at the time of writing, revised exemplar test materials were unavailable but one awarding body was sufficiently concerned to issue a health warning that the old tests should not be used as bench-marks for future tests.

These external tests have a high pass mark, 70 per cent, but they do not contribute to the overall grade a student gets, i.e. they are pass/fail examinations. A student has to pass them to get the GNVQ but the marks they get do not contribute to decisions about the differential grades – merit, distinction – these are made on the basis of the evidence in the student's portfolio. In other words the tests are a hurdle which the student has to jump but they should not be the dominant factor in deciding how you teach. That should be the need for students to generate, independently, evidence of achievement in their portfolios.

KEY IDEA: Teaching to the external tests will not enable your students to gain the higher grades at GNVQ.

Each optional vocational and additional vocational unit taken may need an **internally devised test** to confirm students' knowledge and understanding of the range statements. There is no test specification for these optional units. The tests are subject to external verification by the awarding bodies.

3.2 EVIDENCE

The key to in-course GNVQ assessment is getting students to generate evidence and then judging that evidence using the criteria specified in the GNVQ units. Some general points are worth making before examining that process in some detail in the next section.

Authenticity and validity of evidence

The sort of evidence that can be used for internal continuous assessment is shown in Table 3.1 whilst the methods for collecting it are shown in Table 3.2. Whichever sort of evidence is being considered it has to be authentic and must be collected using valid assessment methods.

Authenticity refers to whether the evidence has genuinely been produced by the student being credited with the achievement and not by someone else. Did this student really draw that picture, complete that task on work experience and so on. If students are working in groups, as they often do, this can be quite a subtle problem and you may need to engage in quite detailed questioning and observation to establish exactly who did what and what achievements can, therefore, be legitimately credited to which individual.

Table 3.1 *Evidence. The following list demonstrates the wide variety of evidence that students could present to demonstrate their achievement in GNVQs (From* Assessing Core Skills, *NCVQ, 1994)*

Written	**Visual**	**3D**	**Oral**
Report	Display	Model	Performance
Diary	Map making	Sculpture	Role play
Log	Storyboard	Produce	Recorded discussion
Essay	Test paper	Artefact	Recorded conversation
Story	Photograph	Product	Interview
Questionnaire	Decoration		Debate
Letter	Graph		Presentation
Notes/Draft	Printout		Commentary
Newspaper	Demonstration		
	Picture		
	Poster		
	Diagram		
	Film		
	Video		

Table 3.2 *There are two main types of evidence you can use in judging a candidate's performance*

Performance evidence	**Supplementary evidence**
generated through:	generated through:
• observation of student performing an activity, e.g. giving a presentation	• oral or written questioning of the student
• scrutiny of something the student has produced, e.g. a video, drawing, etc.	• internal and external tests
• scrutiny of written materials, e.g. a project or assignment	

NCVQ (1993b) recommends that authenticity can be established by the following means:

- directly observing students undertaking an activity
- questioning students as they undertake an activity
- checking claims made by students with third parties, e.g. work experience supervisors, other students and so on
- questioning students on things they have completed recently

- questioning students on how they would do things in the future.

Validity refers to using the appropriate assessment method and so producing the evidence which corresponds most closely to the achievement being assessed. For example consider the Intermediate Business Unit Consumers and Customers. Element 3 has as one of its performance criteria 'communicates politely and meets customers' needs'. Attempting to infer whether a student had achieved this activity from a written report would be an invalid method of assessment. Observing the student giving information to a customer, or getting someone else to do it, e.g. a work-place supervisor who then reports to you, and then asking the customer whether the information met their needs, would be a more valid method of assessment.

To ensure that assessment is both authentic and valid a wide range of methods of generating evidence and assessing it will be needed (Tables 3.1 and 3.2). Evidence can come in two forms:

- **performance evidence** generated through activities like an assignment, or something the student has produced, or watching the student do something
- **supplementary evidence** generated through written or oral questioning or tests.

Do not become too hooked on getting students to continually produce vast quantities of written evidence. There are other ways of producing evidence which are equally as valid for reporting on, describing or explaining something, e.g. giving a talk, making a video or audio-taped presentation, which are more interesting and motivating for the student and will provide you with a welcome break from wading through piles of written projects.

Is there sufficient evidence?

Assessing students takes a lot of time so it is important that you and the student know when to stop generating evidence. Teachers can reduce the work-load of assessment by getting students involved in the process of assessment much more than is usual.

KEY IDEA: Assessment in GNVQ should not be a secretive process. A student needs to know what they have to do and why they might have failed to reach the appropriate standard.

However, it may be that students will need several attempts to generate sufficient evidence to show they have successfully completed the activity described in a particular element. Clearly assessment opportunities need to be planned before the course starts so that you and the students both know when they have the opportunity to demonstrate achievement. This is not an easy task.

KEY IDEA: An assessment plan should show students they have several opportunities to generate evidence to demonstrate achievement in a particular unit.

The converse situation, knowing when to stop, is when you are confident, as an assessor, that the student has a good enough grasp of underlying knowledge, understanding and skills to be able to consistently achieve the activity described in an element to the standard specified by the performance criteria. This means judging whether a student has met all the performance criteria across the entire range associated with a particular element. This may involve making multiple assessments, especially if the student is working in undemanding or restricted situations with a lot of support from the teacher.

If, however, a student is demonstrating achievement in a very demanding situation, for example organising a survey of opinion, presenting and explaining the results to a group where the teacher is providing only limited support and they are meeting the performance criteria for the elements being assessed you can be pretty sure they would be able to replicate this achievement in the future. Supplementary evidence in the form of answers to oral questions like 'Why do you think this happened?' and 'How might you do this differently in the future?' will help give you more confidence in your assessment.

The portfolio of evidence

As a candidate generates evidence which is being assessed for the award of a GNVQ it should be 'filed away' in a portfolio of evidence. The portfolio must contain evidence which relates to:

- Mandatory vocational units achieved. The evidence must show that the candidate has achieved all the performance criteria for a particular element and covered the associated range
- Optional and additional vocational units achieved. The evidence must show that the candidate has achieved all the performance criteria for a particular element and covered the associated range

- Core skill units achieved. The evidence must show that the candidate has achieved all the performance criteria for a particular element and covered the associated range
- Grading activity (more about this later)
- Test performances
- Records of assessor judgements and comments.

Such portfolios are going to be large and it is essential for assessment and verification purposes that teachers and students can navigate through them. A portfolio index sheet of some description, which shows where the evidence of achievement is for each unit is going to be essential. The exact form portfolios take will depend on the student and the subject but may include:

- A4 ring binders of written materials
- Large cardboard boxes containing assignments
- Collections of drawings in large art folders
- Videos
- Computer disks

Finding storage space for these portfolios is a major headache for some GNVQ course teams but it is probably better to keep them at the institution rather than leave them to the vagaries of student travel.

3.3 INTERNAL CONTINUOUS ASSESSMENT

This is the process in which teachers are most intimately involved and the one which causes the greatest angst. Evidence from centres, reported by Alison Wolfe (1994), suggests that teachers have found the internal assessment demanding, confusing and time consuming. The extent to which this is due to inherent defects in the system and the extent to which it is due to a lack of experience amongst teachers and appropriate structures within institutions remains to be resolved.

The assessment process

The GNVQ model of the assessment process is derived from that developed by the Training Development Lead Body (TDLB) and incorporated into the TDLB standards. The model, which is shown in Figure 3.1, divides the assessment process into four stages which are discussed below. Notice, however, at this stage:

- the process is cyclical and contains formative elements, the feedback loops which tell students how they are getting on in terms of the standards they are trying to reach
- produces summative outcomes in the form of elements and units which have been passed
- involves a range of people.

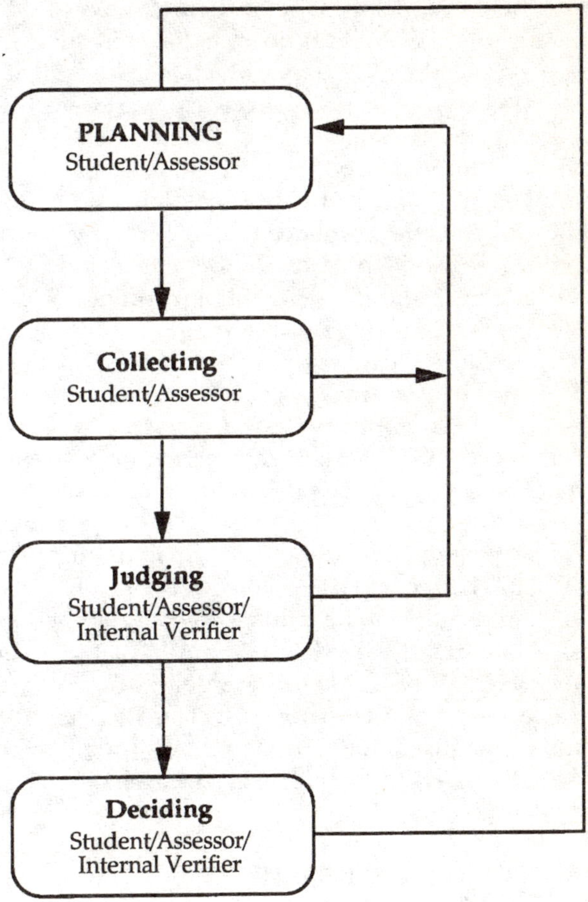

Figure 3.1 *The cyclical process of GNVQ assessment.*

Planning

This involves both the course team and the student. Ideally the course team, after studying the standards in the vocational and core skill units, identify possible opportunities for generating evidence during the learning programme. This results in the production of an assessment map which links assessment opportunities with assessment activities, e.g. assignments. In reality, whilst such a map is essential, teachers are unlikely to have much time to generate it in its entirety before a course starts. None the less such a map is extremely useful and its production should represent a long-term aim of the course team. One of the best ways to do this is to dedicate a wall to it and build it up in half-termly blocks, to begin with, using A3 or A1 sheets of paper which match elements to activities. At the end of the year you have a papered wall which can form the basis of a review meeting.

In the short term you need to produce an assessment plan for the first unit you are going to teach. Such a plan would list the elements to be covered, the evidence the student is going to collect and how you are going to assess it. Bear in mind questions of authenticity, validity and sufficiency when planning the assessment. Look out for gaps in coverage of the range, limited opportunities to generate evidence of achievement and the continual use of similar activities, especially writing, to generate evidence.

Having decided on the assessment activity and what is going to be assessed, you need to list that information on a cover sheet for the activity. Usually this takes the form of an assignment cover sheet (Figure 3.2) which shows the candidate what performance criteria could be met during the activity. It is important that this assessment plan is discussed in depth with the students by the person who is going to assess the evidence generated by the activity: the assessor. Students should then draw up a plan of activities, an action plan, which shows how they are going to generate the evidence for assessment and by what date. This detailed action plan, which is more than just a diary of when things should be handed in by, should be discussed and agreed with the assessor.

3.4 CASE STUDY OF ASSESSMENT

This and subsequent steps in the assessment process can best be illustrated with a case study of one assignment. This case study is intended to demonstrate the process of assessing just one

93205/6 • Issue 1 • June 1993

BTEC GNVQ

Assessment Activity Front Sheet

Name	Date submitted
Centre	Assessor(s)
Assignment title	Portfolio reference number

Tasks	Vocational coverage unit/element/ performance criteria	Evidence produced	Criteria met	Criteria not yet met

Core Skills

Unit	Coverage – Elements/PCs	Criteria met	Criteria not yet met
Communication			
Application of Number			
Information Technology			
Working with Others			
Improving own Learning & Performance			
Problem Solving			

Interim Grading Indications ***(evidence of grading themes)***

Themes	Criteria	Merit	Distinction	Assessor comment
Planning	1	☐	☐	
	2	☐	☐	
Information seeking and information handling	3	☐	☐	
	4	☐	☐	
Evaluation	5	☐	☐	
	6	☐	☐	

Candidate comment	Assessor feedback

Signatures

Assessor Candidate Date

Figure 3.2 *The BTEC Assessment Activity Front Sheet (an example of an assignment cover sheet) being used by the course team in the case study. The other awarding bodies produce equivalent documentation. At the time of writing this documentation was under review.*

assignment. I am not suggesting that the assignment is an exemplary one. In many ways it is rather dull and predictable so few actual details are given. It is the assessment process which is of interest.

The assignment

The way this particular course team had decided to organise their course was very much on a unit by unit basis, starting with the mandatory vocational units. The assignment looked at here was a very substantial one (not all assignments need be this long), designed to provide opportunities to assess all of the fifth mandatory advanced Health and Social Care unit on Health Promotion. To do this successfully meant that the students had to:

- Produce evidence to show they had met the performance criteria for all three elements in the unit
- Demonstrate in their portfolio of work that they had covered the range associated with each element
- Develop the underpinning knowledge and understanding needed to produce the evidence that they had met the performance criteria for each element and to pass the mandatory unit test.

In addition the assignment was a valuable opportunity to develop and demonstrate achievement in core skills, especially communication. Further, the tutors also wanted to use the assignment for grading purposes since there was so much opportunity for students to plan and evaluate their work.

The starting point for this course team, in terms of developing an assignment to cover this unit on Health Promotion, was the knowledge and understanding needed to pass the unit test.

They dissected this out from the unit and test specifications and ensured that the students had covered this first. This meant a substantial amount of 'formal' teaching about major types of risk to health, e.g. drug and solvent abuse, sexually transmitted diseases, HIV, smoking, health and safety at work, identified from the range statements and test specification. In addition to the well-prepared and interesting lectures from their teachers they had also had talks from a worker with a local HIV charity, a health and safety officer from a local company (followed by a visit to the company) a community nurse and a GP. The students were also asked to research topics in the library and to work from textbooks using work sheets.

As a result they were able to build up a considerable body of notes, information leaflets and so on about the major risks to health which they were expected to write up as a word-processed report (stage 1 of the assignment). This gave them the underpinning knowledge and understanding they needed to complete the rest of the assignment and to answer the questions on the mandatory test. Further, the report which the students produced was also planned by the tutors as the main vehicle for assessing the third element of this unit: Identify different types of risk to health. To do this the students had to produce a report which provided evidence that they had met all four of the performance criteria for this element:

1. main risks to health associated with substance abuse are investigated
2. main risks to health associated with unsafe sexual practices are explained
3. main risks to health associated with smoking are explained
4. risks to personal safety within the environment and ways of minimising risk are investigated.

The second part of the assignment involved the students working in small groups to develop a health promotion package for use with a range of different target audiences. These included young children, their fellow college students and workers in a local dye factory, identified from the range statement for these two elements.

This second phase of the assignment began with investigating the demands of presenting health promotion advice to the different target audiences (children, adolescents, adults) within the context of substance abuse, sexual practices, risks to personal safety and smoking (again identified from the range statements). This involved a lot of contact time with a communication specialist and a graphic designer from a local advertising company.

The students studied adverts, posters and promotional leaflets and were asked to produce materials of their own for each of the target audiences for each of the contexts. They were encouraged to use a range of media and to investigate the use of different sorts of audio visual and teaching equipment. All of this was recorded in the form of logbooks, notes, posters, leaflets produced using desktop publishing, video and audio tape, which were stored in a student's portfolio as evidence that they had covered the range for elements 1 and 2 of this unit. It should be emphasised that the quality of the work produced and the variety of media used varied considerably between students since they were working very much on their own at this stage but this was essential if they were to generate evidence that could contribute towards grading.

The students then chose which target audience they wanted to work with and then set about producing their promotional materials in small groups. They were not constrained as to how they presented the materials and they had access to video, reprographic and computer facilities.

The point behind the second part of this assignment was to get them to demonstrate and apply the knowledge and understanding developed during the initial phase of the assignment and to produce evidence that they had met the performance criteria associated with the first two elements of this unit:

- Prepare a plan of health promotion advice
- Present health promotion advice to others.

The performance criteria associated with the second of these elements meant that the students actually had to go and present their material to the target audience, not simply write about it. To do this they needed the underpinning knowledge and understanding about communicating health information and ways of doing it developed from the work with the communications experts.

The final stage of the assignment was for the students to go and present their materials in either a local primary school, the college or the local factory. The arrangements for doing this were left to the students, which added extra components of communication and planning to the assignment. Students were video-taped both practising and giving their presentations and the discussions they had with their tutors about the video tapes were recorded. The video tape contained essential evidence for assessment of both vocational and core skill units.

Organising the students

Whilst this is a fairly routine GNVQ assignment it is none the less enormously complex. Students have to do several things and they can get so caught up in the doing that they forget what they are doing things for. Many get locked on to producing one information leaflet after another, for example, or copying vast chunks of material from text books. Indeed getting students to use media other than written reports to present evidence for assessment is a major problem within GNVQ and one that has drawn some criticism from NCVQ. One of the nice things about this assignment is the variety of ways in which students are producing evidence though it by no means exhausts the possibilities.

KEY IDEA: Assignments should provide opportunities and encourage students to produce evidence for assessment in a variety of different ways. For one thing it makes things more interesting for you.

Clearly then the students need organising, and they need to be taught how to organise their work right from the start of the course so that they have the opportunity to become increasingly independent of you. This independence is essential to achieving the higher grades in GNVQ. This group of students were in the second term of their advanced GNVQ course and some were really good at organising their time. Others were still very weak and needed to be kept to very strict deadlines, i.e. they needed organising. This was reflected in the overall grading of the assignments.

Student planning

The assignment was introduced to all the students together and there was a general discussion of the work which had to be completed in the next five weeks. The elements and performance criteria covered by the assignment were specified on the assignment cover sheet. Considerable time was spent on making sure all the students understood what this meant and how the work they were going to do provided the opportunity for them to present evidence for assessment. This was a genuine discussion led by an experienced teacher but involving all the students who really had got to grips with the GNVQ terminology by this stage and were able to use it to describe and explain what they were going to do. They were also used to this sort of discussion process and they saw the value of it in terms of ensuring they understood what they had to do. Above all, the students were fully aware of the assessment requirements they had to meet and how they might go about meeting the demands. Nothing was hidden: the students knew what they had to achieve.

KEY IDEA: GNVQ assessment should not creep up on students and surprise them from behind. The demands and the evidence needed to demonstrate they have met the demands should be made explicit.

This mature approach had much to do with the induction process (see Theme 3) these students had gone through at the beginning of the course and which was still continuing. This assignment, for example, was going to be used to further develop their understanding of the grading criteria used in GNVQ.

The initial briefing meeting, which lasted an hour, ensured that everyone had a good understanding of the broad details of what they were going to do in the whole assignment and how that related to the GNVQ unit. However, the process of clarification of finer points of detail was on-going and plenty of contact time was available to allow students one to one contact with staff to talk through the work they were doing and whether it was meeting the assessment requirements demanded by the unit. This was an essential part of the assessment process for this team of tutors and, they felt, actually reduced the amount of marking they had to do at the end, since they had a really good idea about the work the students were going to submit as evidence before it was submitted.

Attention was then focused on to the first part of the assignment. This was scheduled to last two weeks giving three weeks to complete the second part of the assignment. In practice they overlapped to some extent. These students had 20 timetabled hours per week for the course, one of which was identified as a tutor period. Fixed points in the timetable for the first two weeks were established. These included the times of lectures and visits. All together these occupied 24 of the possible 38 contact hours in the two-week period. That left 14 contact hours when staff were available to help students on an individual or small group basis. In addition students were expected to work in their own time both in the library and in the open access workshops provided by the college. This gave students the necessary access to computers, help with communication skills, and a multi-skills workshop in which they could make artefacts, videos and so on, needed to support their work.

Action planning

The first task students had to complete was the production of an action plan for the first two weeks of the assignment. This action plan was recorded on the Assessment Activity Action Plan documentation provided by the awarding body (Figure 3.3). The course team were not wholly happy with this but had not yet had time to think about and produce their own planning sheet. They wanted something less complex. The plan was then agreed with the assessor. Again this took time and a lot of discussions. Some students were unrealistic about what they could achieve and some were concerned about identifying resources and so on. Some had still not understood what they needed to do. All of these difficulties were resolved on an individual basis.

Collecting the evidence

Once the tutors had agreed the action plan for each student the programme started. Students attended lectures, went on visits and made notes on the background information required to cover the range statements for the unit. This 'knowledge in first' approach was one which this group of tutors were comfortable with and it was working for them. Other course teams work in different ways.

The amount of material produced by each individual student was enormous. One had a large cardboard box full of posters, folders of written work and her own personal video tape. Sifting through this for evidence of achievement would have been a daunting task. But the intense briefing of the students and their clear understanding of GNVQ resulted in a situation where they could begin to identify the relevant evidence and record where it was located in the portfolio on the portfolio index sheet. This process, whereby students take on more and more of the responsibility for generating and collecting evidence, albeit with the guidance of tutors, is central to making GNVQ assessment feasible.

KEY IDEA: Involving GNVQ students in the assessment process makes GNVQ assessment manageable.

During the time that the students were generating the evidence the course team was monitoring their progress carefully. This enabled them to build up supplementary evidence of achievement, particularly in core skills, through observing students working and questioning them. This was recorded, usually in the form of tick sheets or short, hand-written notes which students attached to their work and so entered their portfolio of evidence.

Judging and deciding

At the end of the allotted time the students handed in that part of the portfolio of evidence which related to the particular unit being

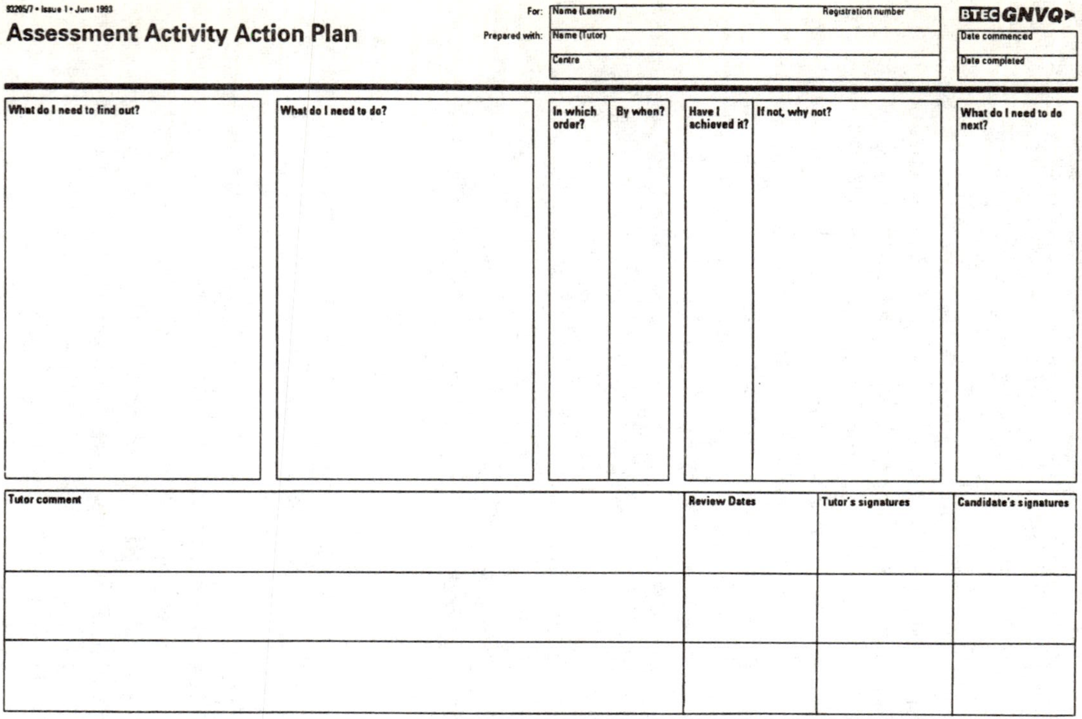

93205/7 • Issue 1 • June 1993

Assessment Activity Action Plan

BTEC GNVQ

For: Name (Learner) — Registration number

Prepared with: Name (Tutor)

Centre

Date commenced

Date completed

What do I need to find out?	What do I need to do?	In which order?	By when?	Have I achieved it?	If not, why not?	What do I need to do next?

Tutor comment	Review Dates	Tutor's signatures	Candidate's signatures

Figure 3.3 *The BTEC Action Planning Sheet being used by the students in the case study. Again the other awarding bodies produce equivalent documentation. At the time of writing this documentation was under review.*

assessed. Even though that did not consist of all the material they had accumulated or produced during the previous five weeks it was still a daunting sight. The evidence submitted had to be assessed three times for:

- achievement in vocational units
- achievement in core skill units
- grading.

Trying to do all three at the same time leads to chaos.

In addition the assessors have to decide whether the evidence presented is valid, authentic and sufficient. For this course team, who had worked closely with the students, monitoring what was going on without necessarily telling students what to do, the issue of validity did not seem problematic. They knew what students had produced because they had seen them producing it. The tutors had also collected a lot of supplementary evidence through observation and questioning which was attached to the students' work. This gave them confidence that they could make valid judgements and decisions. When they needed to check something they asked the students or their internal verifier who became more active during this stage of the assessment process.

Having decided on its validity and authenticity the first task for the assessor was to judge the evidence against the performance criteria. Had the students met all the performance criteria for each element? Where was the evidence? This is essentially a question of detective work which is helped by getting the students to tell you where in their opinion the evidence is and by looking specifically for that evidence. This means that the assessor in this case was not going through the assignments line by line but skimming, looking for specific evidence and then judging it against the performance criteria. All the performance criteria for each element have to be met if the students are going to pass the unit.

KEY IDEA: Whether evidence is adequate for a student to be awarded achievement in a particular element must be judged using the performance criteria.

This process is not one of box-ticking either. It involves making judgements about the evidence presented using the performance criteria and the range to ensure the student has achieved the activity specified in the element. Like any process of judgement you tend to get better at it with experience and training. That was certainly true of this course team:

> To begin with I was really worried about my judgement of evidence. But we talked a lot about what we were doing and my colleagues confirmed my judgements during an INSET day on assessment. That gave me confidence. (GNVQ assessor)

It is important to remember that to assess GNVQ work you must have passed the NVQ unit D33 and possibly D32. A new NVQ unit in this series is currently being developed for GNVQ assessors. More details can be found in the book by Ollin and Tucker (1994).

KEY IDEA: Becoming a proficient assessor of GNVQ work takes time and training.

If the evidence to satisfy a performance criterion could not be found the assessor would then discuss this with the student. Sometimes this discussion would produce the evidence through the student's answers to questions, sometimes the student would go away to do a bit more work, sometimes the assessor and the student agreed that the required standard had not been reached in this assignment.

When they first started, this course team had been worried that students were almost always having to take their assignments away to 'do a bit more', a process they called referral, during the judging and deciding phase. They had realised that this was happening because they were spending too much time on formal classroom teaching and not enough on monitoring work in progress and ensuring that students knew what they had to do. They have now changed their style, as a result of course team discussions, so that whilst they still do a substantial amount of formal classroom teaching, they spend much more time talking with students about work in progress. As a result the rate of referral, sending students off to do a bit more, has dropped.

Recording achievement

After the initial assessment procedure, the candidates' achievement in relation to the vocational units was then recorded on the assignment cover sheet and the assignments were sent off to the core skill specialists for assessment of core skills. This followed a similar pattern of searching for evidence, discussion with student and recording of achievement, with the student, on the assignment cover sheet.

The assignment was then sent back to the assessor for grading, considered in the next section. Finally the assignment was returned to the student, who is able to discuss the comments, always given in terms of the GNVQ unit specifications with both the assessor and the personal tutor. If students are unhappy about the assessment they can appeal using the college appeals procedure. This has been set up using the BTEC code of practice.

KEY IDEA: All GNVQ courses must have an official appeals process.

This whole assessment process took about two weeks, was labour intensive and wearing but did provide the student with quality feedback: they knew exactly how they were getting on, where they needed to make improvements and so on. The amount of paper work was also daunting at first sight but much of it was being completed continually rather than in a great burst at the end. 'You have got to keep on top of the paper work otherwise it gets on top of you.' (GNVQ Business teacher)

The key piece of paper for this course team was the assignment cover sheet which they used to record practically all their assessment comments. This reduced the paper work enormously and helped the students to manage the portfolio. Paper work is examined again in the next chapter.

Verification

Once the assignments had been assessed they were subjected to internal verification. This was carried out by one of the college's internal verifiers. A sample of assignments was taken and the judgement of the assessors checked, effectively by double marking. Any doubts the verifier had were cleared up by questioning both the assessors and the students.

The results of the internal verification, and any lessons to be learnt from it, were disseminated back to the course team during one of their regular review meetings. That the system was working well in this college was confirmed by the external verifier. However, the staff involved were all very experienced and their college had provided a lot of time during the pilot stage of GNVQ for course development. The system was not perfect and was still being altered as the team gained experience. In particular they wanted to refine the record-keeping system. It was also very hard work and they all recognised the need for more time but realised they were not going to get it.

They had gained some extra time for assessment-related activities by the tactic of changing from a preponderance of formal classroom teaching to a more varied diet which included more seminar and tutorial-type work with students. Some of the course team were not happy about this since they felt inadequately prepared for teaching in these new ways and were concerned about 'covering the content'. None the less by working together as a team and by learning from each other they had developed an approach to GNVQ which produced enormously well-motivated students who were succeeding.

KEY IDEA: Assessing GNVQs is a demanding, complex process. Do not underestimate the difficulty of developing an effective assessment regime.

3.5 GRADING

This process has caused more concern than anything else amongst the GNVQ teachers I have spoken with. On reflection I think the problems have largely been caused by three things:

- a change in practice – teachers were not used to grading in this new way and using laid-down criteria
- difficulty in interpreting and operationalising the language of the grading themes and criteria
- a reluctance to let the students go, to let them work in the independent ways needed to generate evidence for grading.

The grades

A student who has passed all the required vocational and core skill units for a particular level of GNVQ will automatically be awarded a pass grade. The achievement of such a grade should not be sneered at: GNVQs are tough qualifications. To gain the higher grades of merit and distinction the candidate's portfolio must contain evidence which meets criteria laid down by the NCVQ. To get a merit, one-third of the work in the portfolio must meet the criteria for the merit grade and to get a distinction one-third of the work must meet the distinction criteria.

Grading themes and criteria

This is where the problems for teachers start. Many are used to judging the quality of a piece of work by a subjective assessment of the way in which students have covered and understood the content which has been taught. GNVQs are graded using quite explicit criteria to do with:

- Grading Theme 1: planning – Foundation, Intermediate and Advanced GNVQ
- Grading Theme 2: information-seeking and information handling – Foundation, Intermediate and Advanced GNVQ
- Grading Theme 3: evaluation – Advanced GNVQ only.

A fourth grading theme is now being introduced which takes account of the quality of the work produced in terms of its vocational content. There has also been some concern amongst employers and higher education tutors that it is the overall award judged on all the evidence in the portfolio which is graded, not individual units as was the case with BTEC diplomas, for example.

You will find details of the grading themes and grading criteria for Intermediate and Advanced GNVQ in Tables 3.3 and 3.4. The grading criteria for Foundation GNVQ vary slightly from those for Intermediate and they can be found in the back of the booklets from the awarding bodies which specify the foundation units. The point here is to try to understand what the criteria mean and how they can be applied.

Interpreting the criteria

Look at the grading criteria for Theme 1: planning in Tables 3.3 and 3.4. The first point to notice is that candidates have to draw up plans **independently**. If you look through all the grading criteria this notion of independence is either explicit or implicit in all of them.

KEY IDEA: To gain merits and distinctions students must be working independently.

This mean that if teachers are giving the students too much help, either in the way they specify the assignment, or in spoon-feeding them information or by providing all the references to materials, for example, then they cannot gain the higher levels of the award. Care also needs to be taken that you are making valid judgements of evidence generated by group. Supplementary evidence is likely to be needed and your assessment plans should take account of this.

Table 3.3 *Grading themes and criteria for Intermediate GNVQ*

	Merit	Distinction
Theme 1: Planning: the way the candidate approaches and monitors the tasks/activities undertaken during a period of learning		
1. Drawing up plans of action	Candidate independently draws up plans of action for a series of discrete tasks. The plans prioritise the different tasks within the given time period	Candidate independently draws up plans for complex activities. The plans prioritise the different tasks within the given time period
2. Monitoring courses of action	Candidate independently identifies points at which monitoring is necessary and recognises where revisions to courses of action are necessary. Appropriate revisions to plans are made with guidance from teacher/tutor	Candidate independently identifies points at which monitoring is necessary and recognises where revisions to courses of action are necessary. Appropriate revisions to plans are made independently
Theme 2: Information-seeking and information-handling: the way the candidate identifies and uses information sources		
3. Identifying information needs	Candidate independently identifies information requirements for a series of discrete tasks	Candidate independently identifies the information requirements for complex activities
4. Identifying and using sources to obtain information	Candidate independently accesses and collects relevant information for a series of discrete tasks. Candidate identifies principal sources independently and additional sources are identified by teacher/tutor	Candidate independently accesses and collects relevant information for complex activities. Candidate uses a range of sources, and justifies their selection

Table 3.4 *Grading themes and advanced criteria for Advanced GNVQ*

Theme 1: Planning: the way the candidate approaches and monitors the tasks activities undertaken during a period of learning

	Merit	Distinction
1. Drawing up plans of action	Candidate independently draws up plans of action for a series of discrete tasks. The plans prioritise the different tasks within the given time period	Candidate independently draws up plans for complex activities. The plans prioritise the different tasks within the given time period
2. Monitoring courses of action	Candidate independently identifies points at which monitoring is necessary and recognises where revisions to courses of action are necessary. Appropriate revisions to plans are made with guidance from teacher/tutor	Candidate independently identifies points at which monitoring is necessary and recognises where revisions to courses of action are necessary. Appropriate revisions to plans are made independently

Theme 2: Information-seeking and information-handling: the way the candidate identifies and uses information sources; and checks and establishes the validity of the information obtained from those sources

3. Identifying and using sources to obtain relevant information	Candidate independently identifies, accesses and collects relevant information for a series of discrete tasks. Candidate identifies principal sources independently and additional sources are identified by the teacher/tutor	Candidate independently identifies, accesses and collects relevant information for complex activities. Candidate uses a range of sources, and justifies their selection
4. Establishing the validity of information	Candidate independently identifies information which requires checking for validity. Candidate checks validity of information using given methods	Candidate independently identifies information which requires checking for validity. Candidate independently selects and applies appropriate methods for checking validity

Table 3.4 *continued*

Theme 3: Evaluation: the way the candidate retrospectively reviews: the activities undertaken; the decisions taken in the course of that work; examination of alternative courses of action that they might have adopted; and examination of the implications of particular courses of action

5. Evaluating outcomes and alternatives	Candidate judges outcomes against original criteria for success; identifies alternative criteria than can be applied in order to judge success of the activities	Candidate judges outcomes against original criteria for success and identifies and applies a range of alternative criteria in order to judge success of the activities
6. Justifying particular approaches to tasks/activities	Candidate justifies approach used; indicates that alternatives were identified and considered	Candidate justifies approach used, basing justification on a detailed consideration of relevant advantages and disadvantages. Alternatives and improvements are identified

Of course, at the beginning of a course students will need more help but you need to plan into your programmes, from the beginning, the opportunities for students to develop, practise and be given feedback on the skills of planning, information-seeking and, in the case of advanced GNVQ students, evaluating their work so that in the later stages of the course they can be consistently producing evidence which meets the grading criteria. Very often students will need to be taught how to do this and deeply held views in both teachers and students about the nature of teaching and learning may need to be challenged.

KEY IDEA: In order to produce evidence for assessment against the grading criteria students will need to develop skills in planning and prioritising, monitoring and revising plans, identifying, accessing and collecting information, checking validity of information, evaluating and justifying approaches. This skill development needs to be started early in the course.

Furthermore these skills need to be developed in a vocational context. Simply providing the students with a one-off study skills module is unlikely to produce the desired outcomes.

The major differences between the merit and distinction grades are the extent to which:

- students demonstrate abilities listed in the grading criteria with or without **guidance**
- students demonstrate abilities of dealing with **discrete tasks** or **complex activities.**

For example an Intermediate student would gain a merit in criterion 2 in Table 3.3 if they 'monitor and revise action plans with guidance' but a distinction if they 'monitor and revise action plans independently'. In criterion 3 for the Advanced GNVQ, merit candidates are independently identifying, accessing and collecting relevant information for a series of discrete tasks whilst the distinction candidate is doing this for a complex activity.

The difference between complex activities and discrete tasks is more imagined than real: they really grade into each other (Table 3.5) but two examples from the case study discussed above may help to realise the distinction. Clearly the second part of the assignment, where the student has to research, develop and present health promotion advice is a complex activity but one which is made up of a number of discrete tasks. It is the way that the two

Table 3.5 *A comparison of discrete tasks and complex activities. The two categories tend to grade into each other*

Discrete tasks	Complex activities
A single-stage task, e.g. type a report A straightforward task, e.g. find a standard resource A task demanding limited application of skills necessary for a complex activity, e.g. only a few of the skills listed opposite are being used	An activity which consists of a series of tasks but which is more than just a sum of their parts since the tasks are interdependent e.g. organising a survey and reporting back on findings Such activities will require the use of related skills: • planning, scheduling, prioritising • identifying information needs and sources • obtaining relevant information • analysis and evaluation • drawing conclusions • self evaluation

students discussed below tackled this part of the assignment that enables you to differentiate between merit and distinction in the first grading theme.

Student A

This student produced an action plan for this part of the assignment independently of the teacher and started work. After three days she grew concerned that she was running behind schedule and discussed this with her teacher. As a result of this discussion, which was recorded in the form of a brief note attached to the action plan, the student modified her plans so they became more manageable. She spent a lot of time researching aspects of advertising and display work and collected a large range of health promotion materials from local and national agencies. She also interviewed health promotion professionals and, on the advice of her teacher, consulted government reports and articles from journals which she ordered through the library. On the basis of her reading she developed a health promotion programme for the local infant school. She was able, after giving her presentation to the children, and setting up her display to discuss with her tutor why she had made the decisions she had, what had gone well and what changes she would make in the future if she were to do this again.

Student A is providing a range of authentic evidence which can be validly judged against the grading criteria. She was thought to be operating at:

- distinction level in the planning theme – she is drawing up plans independently and asking for monitoring when necessary. She then revises her plans independently
- merit level in the information-seeking theme – she has identified and collected information from principal sources but is still being guided towards additional sources
- pass level in the evaluation theme – whilst she is identifying success in general terms she was not really doing so against criteria she had drawn up for success nor had she identified alternative criteria, though alternatives for improvement were being identified.

Overall this student had produced an excellent piece of work but it had not met all the grading criteria for all the grading themes. In a subsequent review session this student discussed this point with her tutor at length and so gained a much better understanding of the grading criteria and identified areas where she needed to develop further skills. This process of reflecting on the grading criteria and what they mean was one of the original aims of the course team in setting this project. Again the important point to notice is that the student has to be judged by the criteria set out and not by the more subjective judgement of 'this is a good piece of work'. Of course any judgmental process has subjective elements but the assessor has to be able to justify the decisions they come to by reference to the grading criteria.

The final grading decisions on each criterion were then recorded on the assignment cover sheet by the assessor and transferred to the portfolio index by the student.

Student B

This student had developed the skills of independent planning to some extent but she found it difficult to plan for the whole of this complex activity. She was helped by the teacher to break it down into a series of discrete tasks which she then planned for independently. She found an enormous wealth of resources in collaboration with other members of the group she was working with though her main contribution was to collect information from the local health authority. As a group the students produced an interesting display for a local factory on the risks to health but on being asked this student thought they would have done better to have given a talk as well. The student met all the performance criteria for the unit but there was some concern about the validity of the assessment given that this group of students had worked so closely together.

This time the assessment for the three grading themes was merit, pass, pass. Again a useful discussion ensued in which this student actually became quite indignant that she had not received higher grades. The internal verifier was asked to intercede and together the assessor, student and internal verifier worked out a plan of action, which involved some extra work, to improve this student's grades in the future. In particular she was helped to realise the difference between complex and discrete tasks, how to break down complex activities by herself by sequencing tasks, and how to monitor her own work better. She commented afterwards:

> I was really disappointed about my marks but I did understand why I had not done well. Now I know what I have to do much better ... I've really had to think about what I am doing though. That helps.

This notion of helping students to think about what they are doing and trying to achieve is, I believe, one of the strongest cases to be made for the GNVQ assessment system. They cannot sit around like sponges and teachers cannot spoon-feed them with information if they are going to get the higher GNVQ grades. Indeed they cannot really pass the qualification if they are just spoon-fed.

KEY IDEA: To satisfy the grading criteria students must become active participants in the GNVQ programme, who think about and plan their own learning.

Students who achieve these higher grades of merit and distinction are accomplished learners who have developed skills which will stand them in good stead for the rest of their lives. For teachers interpreting the grading criteria and using that interpretation to judge evidence presented by their students is not easy, but experience and training help.

Chapter 4

Writing Assignments and Controlling Paper

The main points covered in the last three chapters are:

- GNVQs are complex qualifications which are going to take time and effort to understand
- Both learning programmes and assessment programmes need to be carefully planned
- Students need to be intimately involved with the processes of learning and assessing
- Students need to be taught the skills of independent working early on in the course
- The main approach to teaching must be through assignments on which students work with decreasing support from teaching staff
- Assessing GNVQs is a complex process which involves making and justifying judgements about evidence using specified criteria rather than subjective feeling
- Record-keeping is absolutely essential and students need to be involved with this in order to make it manageable.

Of all these constraints that you need to take into account when beginning to plan and teach a GNVQ the two most important at this stage are the need to base your teaching around assignments and managing the paper flow. This short chapter just deals with some ideas on how to write assignments and how to avoid being overwhelmed by the bureaucracy of GNVQ early on in the course. As you gain experience you can then begin to deal with additional constraints identified in this and the next two themes.

4.1 WRITING ASSIGNMENTS

There is no magical formula for writing a GNVQ assignment. The way you put one together does, however, depend upon how you intend to teach your course. If the decision is to teach on a unit by unit basis then the assignments will tend to have a more limited scope than if you are intending to teach on a thematic basis, when you may cover elements from more than one unit in an assignment. If you are just beginning then it is probably better to start with a unit by unit approach. It is also a good idea to make the first assignments you write ones that can be completed rapidly. This gives both you and the students feedback.

A model

The model shown in Figure 4.1 is one that City and Guilds (1993) has suggested as a useful way of thinking about devising a GNVQ assignment. It is not the only way of doing it but it is a useful starting point. The process appears more mechanical than it actually is. Often teachers just have good ideas, or they want to write an assignment which makes use of a particular feature of the local context, say a hospital, or perhaps they are presented with an idea by a local industrialist. None the less the model does show some important features of a good GNVQ assignment. After you have written an assignment ask yourself:

- is it vocationally relevant and interesting? Would you like to work on it?
- does it allow students to collect evidence and demonstrate achievement in a range of ways (see Tables 2.1 and 3.1)?
- does it address the elements, performance criteria and the range of specified units and is this information being given to the student?
- does it take account of the evidence indicators?
- does it develop core skills which are also identified to the candidate (more about this in the next theme)?
- does it allow scope for students to work independently on planning, information-seeking and evaluating their work (in the case of advanced students) and so provide opportunities for achievement of grading criteria?

Published schemes

There is now a range of publications containing materials which are supposed to be GNVQ assignments. These can provide useful exemplars to work from but you should be careful about using them uncritically. They were designed by individuals working in particular institutions and take account of the constraints operating

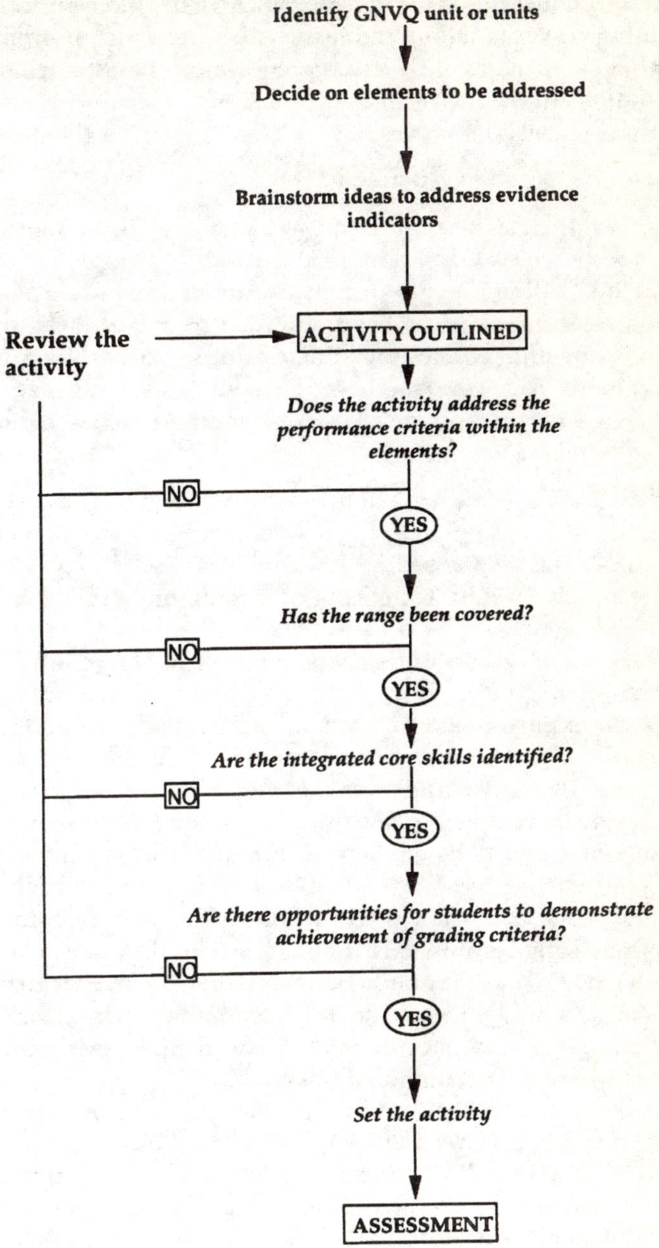

Figure 4.1 *One possible approach to designing an assignment. The process is usually less mechanical than this and you may start with a good idea rather than with the units as suggested here.*

within those institutions. These are likely to be different from those operating in yours. None the less there is no point in reinventing the wheel and many of these assignments can be used, albeit often with modification.

What makes a good assignment?

This is a difficult question to answer. I have seen the same assignment used with two different groups produce completely opposite effects: motivating one group and turning the other off completely. A good assignment at the beginning of a course is likely to be different from one at the end. For example an early assignment should be shorter, covering fewer elements and performance criteria than a later assignment. However, good ones do seem to share a set of common features:

- they set the work to be done in a vocational context. This can be done by using a problem to be solved, e.g. conducting an opinion survey; by setting it within a case study, e.g. a day in a life of a laboratory technician or a community nurse; by asking the student to take on a role, e.g. of someone in an office; using scene-setters of real situations, e.g. a design brief; investigations of places of work, e.g. a nursing home or a factory. Work experience and visits are also good bases for assignments. Whatever else you do make sure the assignment relates to the GNVQ the student is studying!
- they make reasonable demands on the student in terms of both time and knowledge. There is little point in setting an assignment which is so abstract or requires so much background knowledge that the student has little chance of completing it successfully. Failing just dents a student's self-esteem. This does not mean that an assignment should not make cognitive demands, indeed as a student proceeds through a course these demands should become greater and greater: it is just there is little point in making them impossible.
- assignments set early on in the course are designed to be completed rapidly, perhaps in just a few hours or a day, and address a very limited range of elements, perhaps just one. The students need rapid feedback at this stage so they learn about the language of GNVQ. If you give them too much they get overwhelmed. Once they have learned the language of GNVQ they speed up and you will cover more ground.
- the actual assignment specification itself does not contain vast

quantities of information. Often it may consist of the assignment cover sheet and perhaps two or three sheets of A4 paper. These set the scene, give the student an idea of what they have to do and perhaps point to ways of doing it. There may also be supplementary background information and data. This approach serves to prevent the student being intimidated by a vast slab of paper and gives them plenty of scope to work towards and achieve the grading criteria. You can always provide supplementary material later.

- an assignment cover sheet is attached to the front of the assignment which clearly identifies the elements the assignment can provide evidence for. Good cover sheets also have space for recording achievement and comments. They form the backbone of the recording and assessment system.
- they allow students to demonstrate achievement in a number of ways and not just writing. If you give three assignments in a row which simply ask for a word-processed report your students will get pretty fed up and so will you from reading them. Use a bit of imagination and Table 2.1.
- encourage students to work in a range of ways (alone; in small groups) with a range of people (fellow students; teachers; outside experts) using a range of resources (books; film; computers; materials).

4.2 MANAGING THE PAPER CHASE: INITIAL STEPS

By now you will have realised that teaching and assessing GNVQs is a demanding and quite complex task. It is therefore imperative that you produce some sort of learning and an assessment plan for the course. This means identifying on a learning activity by learning activity basis exactly what the assessment opportunities are and how they map on to the vocational units. You will also need to do this for the core skill units (see Theme 2). This is a gargantuan task for a whole course and will take time but it is absolutely essential if you are not going to get swamped by the process, but take it slowly.

What paper work do I need?

To support your planning you need an administrative system. It's no good pretending this is not the case, that managing the flow of paper is unimportant. One of the benefits of the national curriculum in primary schools, for example, has been a great improvement in record-keeping. The trick is to do enough and not too much. Figure 4.2 will give you an overview of how one awarding body sees the flow of information.

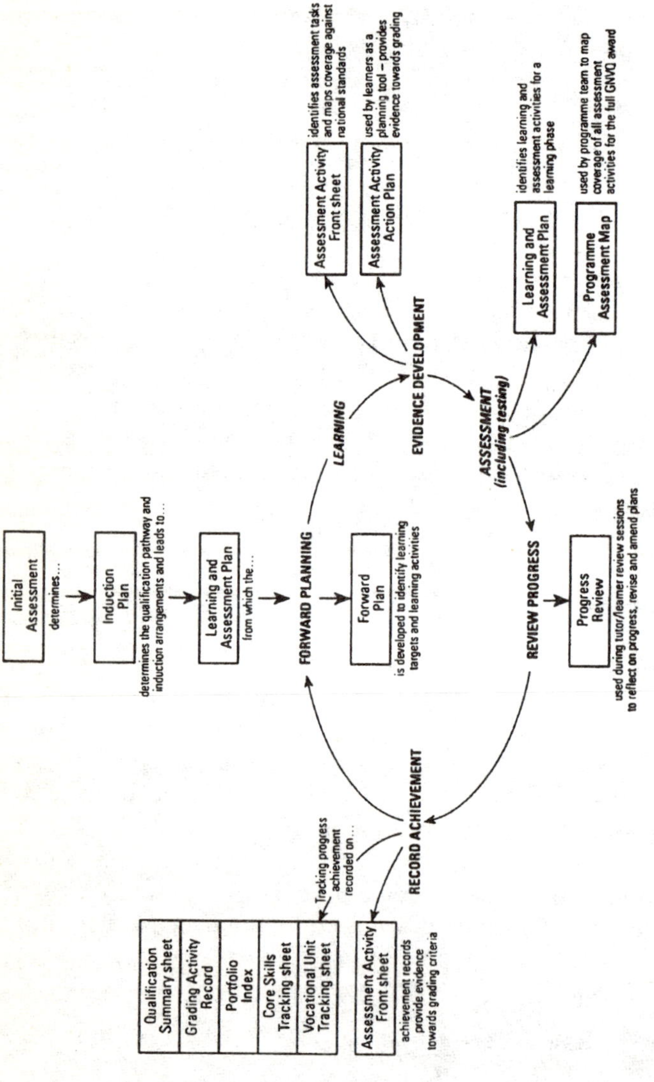

Figure 4.2 *Managing the flow of information. BTEC's suggested approach to recording and planning. The boxes represent individual blank documents provided by BTEC. Other awarding bodies supply similar documentation. At the time of writing this documentation was being updated. Further information can be obtained directly from BTEC.*

All the awarding bodies produce recording documentation and, whilst this is way over the top in terms of the amount of paper it generates, you would be well advised to use it in the first instance. As you gain experience you will discard some of the record-keeping machinery since you do not actually need it, though interestingly which bits are discarded varies between institutions. You will also adapt the awarding bodies' documentation to meet your needs. Figure 4.3 shows how BTEC sees its record-keeping system meshing together. The claim is that this system facilitates:

- the identification of the learning pathway
- the planning of learning and assessment
- the monitoring and reviewing of learner progress
- the recording of formative and summative achievement
- the recording of formative grading recommendations
- the tracking of learner progress
- the location of evidence for purposes of internal and external verification (BTEC (1993a) p66)

A basic system

In the fullness of time you will be able to cope with this list and Figures 4.2 and 4.3 though I suspect you will have modified the system to your own purposes. To start with you need a much more basic system. On the evidence development side:

- an assignment cover sheet which identifies tasks and maps coverage against the units, and on which you can record your assessments
- an assignment activity action plan which the students can use to plan their work.

On the recording side:

- a decent portfolio index which students can use to record the evidence they have submitted and their achievements.

The rest you can add in slowly, say vocational and core skill tracking sheets after the first half-term when students are beginning to make real progress. If you are not involved with student induction or personal tutoring then forget about those bits of the recording system until you have built up your expertise in teaching the vocational and core skill units.

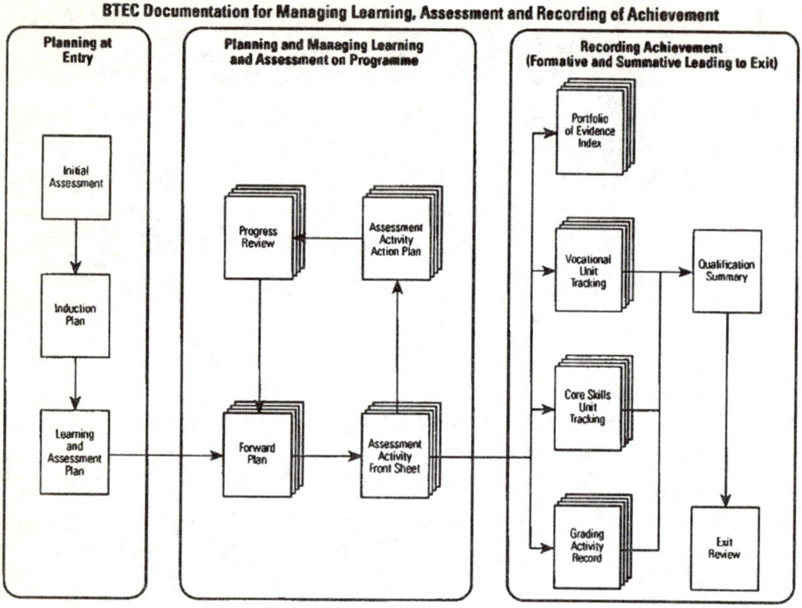

Figure 4.3 *Managing the flow of information. The documents supplied by one awarding body, BTEC, to help with managing learning, assessment and recording achievement. You may only need to deal with a small subset of this documentation, or its equivalent supplied by the other awarding bodies, in the first instance. At the time of writing this documentation was being updated. Further information can be obtained directly from BTEC.*

KEY IDEA: Develop your expertise with GNVQ slowly. Try and understand one thing thoroughly before you move on. Try and resist attempts to get you to take on too much.

However it is easy to go the other way and just rubbish the processes of recording student achievement as being irrelevant to the job of teaching. It is not, since by clearly identifying and recording what your students have achieved, you will motivate them. For many GNVQ students simply recognising what they have achieved may be a new experience and one which has a salutary effect on their self-esteem. The recording also gives you an opportunity to talk with them about what they are doing, where they need extra help and what they are going to do next.

Theme 2:

Core Skills

GNVQs are intended to offer a broad education as a foundation for both further education and training leading to employment. To ensure the breadth of the qualification students have to complete not only the vocational units required for an award but also core skill units. All GNVQs must incorporate the core skill units in three areas:

- **Communication**
- **Application of Number**
- **Information Technology**

These are the **mandatory core skill units** with specifications accredited by NCVQ but certificated by the awarding bodies.

In addition it is recommended that students take two additional core skill units:

- **Personal skills – improving own learning and performance**
- **Personal skills – working with others**

These are the **additional core skill units** with specifications accredited by NCVQ but certificated by the awarding bodies. A final core skill unit in **problem solving** has been developed but at the time of writing was still waiting to be accredited. However, achievement in this core skill, which is identified as crucial by employers, can be recorded in the National Record of Achievement.

Questions about core skills are legion but the ones addressed in this theme relate directly to the mandatory GNVQ core skill units including:

- **How are GNVQ core skills specified?**
- **What do students have to learn and achieve?**
- **How are core skills assessed?**
- **How can core skills be taught?**

Chapter 5

Introducing GNVQ Core Skills

The purpose of this and the next chapter in this theme is to help you familiarise yourself with the GNVQ core skill units at levels 1, 2 and 3. Even though you may have been asked to teach only one of the units (or none!) it is still worth while getting an overview of the core skill requirements that your students have to achieve. Indeed you may find that as a result you realise you have an important contribution to make to the teaching of core skills.

5.1 GETTING TO KNOW THE UNITS: A STRATEGY

A process recommended by NCVQ for familiarising yourself with the units involves:

- reading the unit specifications at the level demanded in the programme on which you are teaching, e.g. Level 2 for an Intermediate GNVQ, Level 3 for an Advanced GNVQ, and making a note of the things and statements which need clarification
- participating in a programme of meetings to discuss and clarify understanding of the units. These meetings should focus on understanding of units, not discussing details or problems of implementation. Whilst it is difficult to do this the advice is sound. It is to easy to get side-tracked at this stage into asking questions like 'How am I going to do this?' rather than first getting an overview of what your students have to do and achieve.

This process is undoubtedly time-consuming but if you can sort out problems of understanding and generate a common understanding as to the meaning of the statements in the core skill units at the outset then later processes, for example assessment of core skills, become less problematic. Your internal and external verifiers are likely to be key people in helping to clarify meaning.

KEY IDEA: It is essential to develop a common understanding of the core skill unit specifications and their meaning amongst members of a course team.

Whilst the advice from NCVQ and from the awarding bodies about the need for familiarisation with the core skill units at the level you are teaching is sound, experience suggests that you will find it helpful to familiarise yourself with how the elements of achievement, performance criteria and range statements change, systematically, as the level of achievement in each core skill unit increases. To help with this more complex process the next chapter contains a lot of tabulated material. Essentially this consists of a reorganisation of the existing mandatory core skill specifications so that you can see details of the structure of the units which is not so evident when you look at the original specifications. (You should, however, ensure that you have a copy of these specifications: they are at the back of the books which contain the vocational unit specifications.)

In particular, the tables bring out the differences between the way different mandatory core skill units are specified and their nested, internal structure. The deeper understanding of the core skill units this provides will help you later to appreciate how core skills are assessed and help you see how you can meet the need for progression in the teaching of core skills. The remainder of this chapter is concerned with some more general aspects of the GNVQ core skill units.

(N.B. If you do not understand the following terms: element; performance criteria; range; evidence indicator, read Chapter 1 before proceeding.)

5.2 SPECIFICATION OF CORE SKILLS

The GNVQ core skill units are specified in the same way as the vocational units using:

- elements of achievement (which describe what the student has to achieve)
- performance criteria (which provide a means of judging successful achievement for each element)
- range statements (which describe the range of settings or contexts in which the activity should be performed successfully and the range of techniques which students should master).

There are no evidence indicators for the mandatory core skills units as the evidence should come from work being undertaken to meet the requirements of the vocational units.

What students have to achieve to pass the GNVQ core skill units is, therefore, specified explicitly and in detail which means that GNVQ core skills require detailed and explicit assessment. Core skill units have therefore got to be taken seriously because the students have to produce a considerable amount of evidence to pass these units at the level appropriate to the GNVQ they are taking.

KEY IDEA: Students have to pass all of the elements of the mandatory core skill units at the appropriate level by producing evidence which meets the requirements of each performance criteria across the entire range associated with each element to be awarded a GNVQ.

As with the vocational units, it is important to realise that the core skill units are statements of outcomes: they tell you what the student has to achieve in order to pass. Consequently they are not like a traditional syllabus and require, therefore, careful interpretation. In particular the considerable amount of underlying knowledge and understanding needed by the student to demonstrate achievement, and so pass the core skill units, will need to be teased out. Much of that knowledge and understanding will require quite explicit teaching, often by specialist teachers, with considerable support and extra help being provided for weaker students. Two key areas here are basic literacy and numeracy. Ways of teaching and providing support for core skill development are examined in Chapter 7.

Levels of attainment

Each core skill unit has five levels of attainment and there is a separate unit specification for each core skill at each level. As you move up the levels the achievements required of the student become more demanding and the range increases, which means the student has to do more. This is potentially very problematic for intermediate students who, realistically, only have one year in which to develop and demonstrate quite a wide range of skills.

A good example of the progression in demand as the level of achievement increases is afforded by Element 1 of the communication unit:

- Communication 1.1 (Level 1, Element 1): Take part in discussions with known individuals on routine matters
- Communication 2.1 (Level 2, Element 1): Take part in discussions with a range of people on routine matters

- Communication 3.1 (Level 3, Element 1): Take part in discussions with a range of people on a range of matters.

The changes are also reflected by an increase in the demand of the associated performance criteria and an increase in the number of the range statements (see Tables 6.2(a) and 6.3(a)).

KEY IDEA: The higher levels of achievement in GNVQ core skills build systematically on the lower levels of achievement.

5.3 KNOWLEDGE, UNDERSTANDING AND GNVQ CORE SKILLS

GNVQ core skills have been designed to have some correlation with National Curriculum levels of attainment (Table 5.1) though the extent to which this correlation survives after the current revision of the National Curriculum remains to be seen. The relationship is most precise between Mathematics in the National Curriculum and the GNVQ core skill unit, Application of Number. This is why the reference numbers for the relevant attainment targets (ATs) for Mathematics in the National Curriculum have been included in at least some of the performance criteria and range statements for each element of achievement in this core skill unit (see Tables 6.4 and 6.5). The relationship is less strong between the National Curriculum and core skill units in Communication and Information Technology.

Table 5.1 *Correspondence between GNVQ core skill levels and National Curriculum levels of attainment. Read this table with a certain degree of suspicion: the correspondence is on broad equivalence rather than exact correlation. See text for further details.*

GNVQ core skill units levels	National curriculum levels
1	4 and below
2	5 and 6
3	7
4	8 and 9
5	10 and above

The application of knowledge

It is, however, important to realise that the GNVQ core skill units do place emphasis on the application of skills in practical settings, so the relationship between the National Curriculum levels and the GNVQ core skill levels is one of broad equivalence rather than exact correspondence of content. Just as with the vocational units, GNVQ students have got to demonstrate their competence in core skills through achieving outcomes of purposeful activities rather than just showing they know something. Once again, then, the emphasis is not on just knowing something but on knowing what to do with it, i.e. applying knowledge and understanding. It is important to bear this in mind when reading the Application of Number core skill unit in particular.

For example, consider the following elements of achievement:

- Use images to illustrate points made in discussions with a range of people on a range of matters (Communication, Element 3.3)
- Gather and process data (Application of Number, Element 3.1)
- Edit, organise and integrate complex information from different sources (Information Technology, Element 3.2)

To achieve all of these elements requires students to have both underpinning knowledge and understanding about:

- different ways of producing and using images to convey information
- the techniques which can be used to collect and analyse data
- using IT to manipulate different sorts of information, e.g. text, numbers and pictures,

and that they can use them in a vocational setting and produce evidence to show that they are competent in their execution by, for example:

- giving talks to different groups of people in which images, say photographs or graphs on overhead transparencies, are used to illustrate the main points they are making
- collecting data during a survey and analysing it to answer specific questions
- producing reports which contain text, tables of numerical data and graphs of different sorts.

So:

> The Core Skill Units demand application of skills within a vocational context and therefore go beyond the requirements

> within the National Curriculum. The units emphasise the outcomes of purposeful activities, rather than emphasising knowledge. (BTEC (1993a) p60)

Despite the soundness of this statement it is worth reiterating that all these core skills do have underpinning knowledge and understanding which students need to be taught. The point is, helping them develop that knowledge and understanding is a necessary process but not sufficient for demonstrating achievement in the core skills. Students need to demonstrate their knowledge and understanding in a practical way, preferably in the vocational context of the GNVQ they are studying, though this is not always possible. However, simply giving students more and more opportunities for assessment against the core skill criteria, whilst necessary is not likely to be sufficient to help them develop their core skill competence. As with the vocational units a judicious blend of didactic teaching, practice and assignment work is likely to be needed. The trick is getting the balance right.

KEY IDEA: Teaching core skills is going to involve using a range of different methods, approaches and resources.

Language

The examples of elements listed above also illustrate the vagueness of some of the language you are likely to find in the core skill units. What, for example, constitutes 'a range of people', 'a range of matters' and 'complex information from different sources'? What sort of data are students supposed to 'gather and process'?

To sort out the answers to these questions, and to understand what is meant by the elements of achievement, students have to achieve at different levels, you have to use both the performance criteria and the range statements. The extent to which these help you depend on the unit and this is one reason for the extensive tabulations you will find in the next chapter.

So, just like the vocational units, the core skill unit specifications are going to require careful interpretation to ensure that your students are given adequate opportunity to develop underpinning knowledge and understanding necessary to practice and demonstrate their achievement of the core skills in a variety of settings. Furthermore, if you need to spend time understanding and interpreting the units, then so will your students. To help them understand and take core skills seriously it is clearly important that you are confident about the meaning of the units.

5.4 WHAT CORE SKILLS DO STUDENTS HAVE TO DO?

Students taking a particular GNVQ have to complete the mandatory core skill units, Communication, Application of Number and Information Technology at the appropriate level. The minimum requirement for the award of:

- Foundation GNVQ is the achievement of Level 1 in each of the three mandatory core skill units
- Intermediate GNVQs is the achievement of Level 2 in each of the three mandatory core skill units
- Advanced GNVQs is the achievement of Level 3 in each of the three mandatory core skill units.

There is, however, nothing to prevent a student achieving core skills at a level beyond that required for the GNVQ they are taking. Indeed this is one way of adding value to the GNVQ programme. For example many advanced science GNVQ students are working at Level 5 in the Application of Number unit as they complete their assignments. Providing they cover the range they can be accredited with this unit at Level 5.

Implications for student enrolment

The need for students to achieve core skills at the level of the award they are taking has proved difficult for some. For example, some intermediate GNVQ students have found the Application of Number unit at Level 2, in particular, very demanding. This raises two important general points:

- When enrolling students on a course you need to ensure that they have the background knowledge and understanding needed to have a realistic chance of achieving the mandatory core skill units at the required level in the time available for the course. This is especially important for intermediate GNVQ students where the course duration is, realistically, only one year. The relationship between the core skill units and the National Curriculum will help you here. For example students presenting themselves for enrolment on an Intermediate GNVQ course who have some reasonable GCSE grades, say Ds and Es in most subjects but an F or a G in say maths should be a cause for concern. Can such students realistically be expected to improve the level of their performance from National Curriculum level of 4 or less (i.e. Level 1, see Table 5.1) to a

National Curriculum level of 5 or 6 (i.e. Level 2) in one year? The answer is 'possibly' but given the formula for funding by the FEFC of colleges such students do need careful counselling to ensure they are on the right course, both for themselves and the college. For such students it may be best to enrol them on a foundation programme simply to develop their mathematical competence for a year.

- Be prepared to commit time and resources to the teaching of core skills. There is so much to get through in a GNVQ that it is tempting to overlook the core skill units and concentrate on the vocational units. However, a student will not receive the award unless they pass the core skill units. It is worth reiterating, the core skill units must be taken seriously and your students need to be convinced to take them seriously.

Additional core skill units: why do them?

Whilst it is not essential to complete the two additional core skill units, and Personal Development – working with others, and Personal Development – improving your own learning and performance, to achieve the award of a GNVQ, 'many colleges, with experience of GNVQs, have commented on the advantages of developing the core skills in working with others and improving [your] own learning even though they are not required for a GNVQ.' (FEU (1994) p22). Further,

> Colleges which had consulted with employers on the new qualifications found that employers tended to value problem solving and personal skills as highly as communication skills [whilst] another powerful argument came from the college which argued that the optional core skills could have a vital part to play in developing action planning systems. Student centred action planning, review and recording processes are possible only if diagnosis and target setting take place and learning is planned and reviewed. If the student is to be central to these activities, the skills of self analysis, self management and problem solving need to be developed. These are the optional core skills and can be developed as the student is given greater autonomy. (FEU, op. cit.)

The clear implication of this for you is that you must, as a bare minimum, be familiar with the mandatory core skill units at the level of award you are working with, and how achievement at the higher levels of the core skills units builds on achievement at lower levels. However, as your understanding and confidence of working with GNVQ core skills increases you should, perhaps, consider developing assessment opportunities for the optional core skill units and you might also think about increasing the level of the core skill at which some students are working. This is especially important when students already have skills at or above the level of the GNVQ award to which they are working.

Unfortunately space does not permit a detailed examination of the additional core skill units in this book. However, the techniques suggested for dealing with the mandatory core skills in this theme are equally applicable to the additional core skill units.

5.5 COURSE DELIVERY

Practical arrangements for teaching, learning and assessing core skills are of concern to anyone involved with GNVQ. The guidance from both NCVQ and the awarding bodies is unequivocal in this respect:

> Evidence of core skills should be collected from the projects, assignments and activities students complete to meet the requirements of GNVQ vocational units. (NCVQ (1993b) p14)

> Wherever possible core skills should be delivered in an integrated way within a vocational context. Core skills should permeate the learning and assessment activities which make up the GNVQ programme. Vocational activities should be designed to create opportunities for learners to generate and collect evidence which provides comprehensive coverage of core skills. (BTEC (1993a) p60)

> Although specified as separate units, the development of core skills should be integrated with the vocational activities students carry out. It is therefore necessary to ensure that GNVQ learning programmes are designed to create opportunities to demonstrate the achievement of core skills in the context of vocational activities. (RSA (1993) p12)

> Most candidates will be developing their core skills for assessment, and ideally be generating evidence, through vocational activities. This is an integrated approach so that a candidate learns core skills naturally through a vocational context (City & Guilds. (1993) p21)

KEY IDEA: Evidence of core skill achievement should come primarily from vocationally based assignments.

In general this is sound advice: candidates should develop their understanding of core skills and demonstrate them in a vocational context since it is the vocational context which motivates them. Imagine sitting GNVQ students down in a classroom to learn mathematics in the same way they have been learning, and probably doing so poorly, for the past five years. Not only is little learning likely to take place, not only does this go against the whole ethos of GNVQ but you are also likely to have very disaffected students who may well leave. This is bad for the students and bad for the institution, especially FEFC institutions, where the financial penalties for students dropping out are really quite severe. Clearly, then the teaching and development of these core skills needs some careful thought, and ways of integrating them with vocational work will become obvious in later chapters.

However, we do need to put a rider on integration of core skills. As NCVQ point out:

> while it is important to ensure that core skills are delivered and assessed in an integrated way this does not mean losing them without trace in the programme. Although core skills are embedded in tasks and activities, being explicit about them will help people to learn and practice them more effectively. (NCVQ (1993b) p9)

Transferable skills

The problem with integration revolves around issues to do with learning core skills and transferability. If students are going to improve their performance in core skills and transfer that learning to new contexts, they have got to know what core skills they are working with. It is very difficult to improve, say, your communication skills if you do not know which communication skills you are using and if you do not get feedback on how well you are using a particular communication skill.

The message to take on board here is do not take core skills for granted. Do not assume that since you think they are part of everyday life or are integral to the way we do things that students will somehow develop competence in them by some magical, osmotic process. Get them out in the open, get students to look at the units and understand what they have to achieve, get students to take core skills seriously and not avoid them. Identify on cover sheets what core skills students might develop whilst they are working on assignments.

Additional support

Another important rider, regarding teaching support, is provided by the awarding bodies but I do not think they make the point strongly enough. For example:

> Some students, however, may need additional teaching support to develop their core skills before they can apply them within their vocational activities. (Royal Society of Arts (1993b) p13)

I would go further than this and say all students will need some explicit instruction if they are to develop adequately the knowledge and understanding which underlie the core skills.

KEY IDEA: All students are likely to need explicit teaching of the knowledge and understanding underpinning the GNVQ core skills.

This is obvious in some of the core skill units, for example Application of Number, and here the challenge lies in getting the balance between formal teaching and the application of the core skill in a practical setting which is necessary to produce evidence for assessment. However, communication skills and IT also have a theoretical basis which students should learn about. This will help them develop these vital skills to a much higher degree because they will think about what they are doing.

This raises another general question about core skills: who teaches them? Again this question is addressed in the following chapters but two short case studies may help you to get a feel of the possible pitfalls of core skills teaching, learning and assessment.

5.6 CASE STUDIES

These two case studies concentrate on the institutional arrangements made for teaching core skills in GNVQ programmes. The case studies should be interpreted in the spirit in which they are written, i.e. as providing illumination not condemnation. There are many blind alleys in the development of a GNVQ course.

Case 1

This is a classic example of the hegemony of the timetable over institutional arrangements and a lack of understanding of the nature of GNVQ by senior management. This centre had decided to do four intermediate and two advanced GNVQs even though it had no prior experience of running vocational courses. The timetabler had looked through the programmes for these GNVQs and identified the core skills as an element which was common to them all. Consequently the students on all the GNVQs at each level were timetabled for core skills at the same time. The core skills were to be delivered by an English, a maths and an IT teacher in isolation from the vocational context. Since there had been no meetings of all the staff involved in delivering the GNVQ course, at which they had developed common understanding about the core and vocational units and decided their roles in respect to teaching the core skills, chaos ensued. Nobody knew what anybody else was doing and as a result the core skill development amongst pupils was poor. Furthermore students were producing very little evidence of core skill achievement in their vocational work.

Fortunately the deteriorating situation was spotted by the vocational teachers and the verifiers after about a term had passed and the system was patched up. Fundamental change has now taken place including the formation of course teams containing core skill teachers and considerable staff development on the teaching of core skills.

The message here is I think threefold:

- you cannot devolve total responsibility for core skills development to another teacher; it is, like so much else in GNVQ, a team effort
- the team of teachers delivering GNVQ have got to develop a common understanding of the core skill and vocational units and plan the course programme together
- beware senior management who will know less about GNVQ than anybody. You will need to make your case with them about providing time and resources to develop your course.

Case Study 2

This is based on a highly experienced BTEC National Diploma course team who were switching over to GNVQ. Traditionally they had worked in a course team with communication and maths specialists but college cut-backs had put pressure on them to deliver the whole of the GNVQ, including the core skills, by themselves. They had felt confident they could do this but they soon realised they could not. The reasons were threefold:

- the core skills disappeared into the vocational context and whilst students were undoubtedly 'doing' core skills they could not recognise them. Consequently they were not progressing to the higher levels of achievement needed for advanced GNVQ, since they did not have the opportunity to practise and think about their core skill development
- the terminology of the GNVQ core skill units confused the vocational specialists; they did not understand what they were supposed to do
- having resolved the first two points the course team found they did not have the expertise or subject knowledge necessary to teach the knowledge and understanding underpinning the core skills at Level 3.

The original course team has now been reassembled and core skill development is now much better. The message here is:

- do not underestimate the difficulties of the core skill units
- do not overestimate your ability to teach outside your main area without considerable staff development
- value your core skill specialists and involve them in planning the course.

First, though, you need to familiarise yourself with the core skill units, and that is where we turn next.

Chapter 6

The Mandatory Core Skill Units

In this chapter each of the mandatory core skill units is examined in some detail. Much of the material is tabulated, with a commentary being provided on the tables in the text. Each unit is also used to draw out more general features of GNVQ core skills.

Whilst this chapter is mostly concerned with helping you to understand what your students have to do in relation to core skills, an essential task since you are likely to have to explain it to your students, there is also an attempt to help you start thinking about how you might begin teaching core skills. In particular it begins to explore possible mechanisms for integrating core skills into GNVQ vocational programmes. A useful thing for you to do after each core skill has been explored is simply to think about the unit specifications of the vocational units you will be teaching and try to see how these mandatory core skills fit with them. It may be just a particular core skill element of achievement or a part of the range but you might be surprised how many opportunities there are for assessing and developing core skills through the students' vocational work.

6.1 COMMUNICATION UNIT

GNVQ students are expected to demonstrate their achievement in two aspects of communication:

- interpreting language
- using language to present information and ideas,

by speaking, listening, writing and reading. To achieve this the communication core skill units consist of four themes:

- taking part in discussions
- preparing written materials
- using images to illustrate points made in writing and discussion
- reading and responding to written materials and images.

These lead to the four elements of achievement for this core skills unit. As Table 6.1 shows, as you move up the levels (read the table from left to right) the tasks demanded of the students, as expressed in the elements of achievement, increase in complexity. Notice, for example, the movement from 'routine matters' to a 'range of matters' and from 'known individuals' to a 'range of individuals'. To interpret the meaning of these phrases requires the use of the performance criteria (Table 6.2) and, especially, the range (Table 6.3).

Performance criteria

The listing of the performance criteria in Table 6.2 indicates that major jumps in performance are expected as a student progresses from Level 1 to Level 3. To achieve this is likely to take time and, bearing in mind that many students will come with skill levels below Level 1 or not demonstrated at Level 1, it will require practice for the students to achieve the higher levels. Do not assume, therefore, that advanced students, for example, will be working at Level 3 in any core skill from day one of an advanced course. Many will need considerable help to get to the appropriate level of attainment in core skills needed to gain the GNVQ they are working for. Consequently it may well be not until quite late in the course before a student is consistently performing at the required level. This needs to be borne in mind when writing assignments and negotiating targets with students.

KEY IDEA: Progression in development of core skills needs to be planned in to the course.

Another important point is the link between the performance criteria in the communication unit and the grading criteria. As a student moves from Level 1 to Level 3 increasing independence is required. This is well exemplified in the performance criteria for the fourth element where the student is expected at Levels 1 and 2 to use 'the sources provided' but at Level 3 is required to select appropriate 'sources of clarification'. This correlates well with the movement from merit to distinction in the first two grading themes and with the requirements of the extra grading theme of Evaluation introduced at Advanced level.

KEY IDEA: The development of core skills can make a major contribution to the overall grade a student receives and this should be emphasised since it helps students to realise the importance of work in the core skill areas.

Table 6.1 *Elements of achievement for the mandatory core skill unit* **Communication.** *Note that the main points of comparison as you read across the table from right to left are shown in bold italics*

	Level 1	Level 2	Level 3
Element 1	Take part in discussions with ***known individuals*** on routine matters	Take part in discussions with a ***range of people*** on routine matters	Take part in discussions with a range of people on a ***range of matters***
Element 2	Prepare written materials in ***pre-set formats***	Prepare written material on ***routine matters***	Prepare written material on a ***range of matters***
Element 3	Use images to illustrate points made in writing and in discussions with ***known individuals*** on routine matters	Use images to illustrate points made in writing and in discussions with a ***range of people*** on routine matters	Use images to illustrate points made in writing and in discussions with a range of people on a ***range of matters***
Element 4	Read and respond to written material and images in ***pre-set formats***	Read and respond to written materials and images on ***routine matters***	Read and respond to written material and images on a ***range of matters***

Table 6.2(a) *Performance criteria for the* **first element** *of achievement for the mandatory core skill* **Communication.** *Major changes in emphasis as you move up the levels are shown in* ***bold italics***

	Level 1	Level 2	Level 3
Element 1	Own contributions are clear and appropriate to the subject matter	Own contributions are clear and appropriate to the subject matter	***Own contributions are expressed effectively for their purpose and are appropriate to the subject matter***
	Own contributions are made in a tone and manner suited to the audience	Own contributions are made in a tone and manner suited to the audience	Own contributions are made in a tone and manner suited to the audience
	Contributions from others are listened to attentively	Contributions from others are listened to attentively	***Others are explicitly encouraged to contribute and their contributions listened to attentively***
	Own understanding of points made by others is actively checked and confirmed	Own understanding of points made by others is actively checked and confirmed	Own understanding of points made by others is actively checked and confirmed

Table 6.2(b) *Performance criteria for the* **second element** *of achievement for the mandatory core skill* **Communication.** *Major changes in emphasis as you move up the levels are shown in* ***bold italics***

Level 1	Level 2	Level 3
Documents are complete and accurate	***All necessary information is included and information is accurate***	***The fullness and accuracy of information included is appropriate to the purpose and needs of the audience***
Documents are legible	Documents are legible	Documents are legible
Grammar and punctuation follow standard conventions, and words used routinely are spelled correctly	Grammar and punctuation follow standard conventions, and words used routinely are spelled correctly	**Grammar, punctuation and spelling follow standard conventions**
	The format used is appropriate to the nature of ***the material and information is ordered appropriately to maximise audience understanding***	The format used is appropriate to the purpose of the material and information is ordered appropriately to maximise audience understanding

Table 6.2(c) *Performance criteria for the* ***third element*** *of achievement for the mandatory core skill* **Communication**. *Major changes in emphasis as you move up the levels are shown in* ***bold italics***

Level 1	Level 2	Level 3
	Images are used to support main points in the communication	***Images are used to support main points which the audience may have difficulty understanding***
Images selected are relevant to the point(s) made	***Images provide clear illustration of the point(s) to which they refer***	***Images provide clear illustation to the point(s)*** *to which they refer*
Images are used at appropriate places	Images are used at appropriate places/***times***	Images are used at appropriate places/times

Table 6.2(d) *Performance criteria for the* **fourth element** *of achievement for the mandatory core skill* **Communication**. *Major changes in emphasis as you move up the levels are shown in* ***bold italics***

Level 1	Level 2	Level 3
Main points are accurately identified	Main points are accurately identified	Main points are accurately identified
The meaning of unfamiliar words, phrases and images is accurately identified using the sources provided	The meaning of unfamiliar words, phrases and images is accurately identified using the sources provided	***The meaning of unfamiliar words, phrases and images is accurately identified***
		Appropriate sources of clarification are used

The performance criteria for the elements of achievement in the communication unit also emphasises the nested nature of the GNVQ core skills; the higher levels subsume the lower ones. Thus a student working at Level 3 in a core skill is also producing evidence which satisfies Levels 1 and 2. This is important for a student who does not produce sufficient evidence to pass the unit at a higher level since they may have enough evidence to be awarded the unit at the lower level. Whilst this may mean that they do not get the overall GNVQ it is still a positive record of their achievements.

The nested nature of the core skills also gives hints as to how you can plan progression. Start working at the lower levels with more directed tasks and then slowly increase the amount of autonomy you give the student. This is also a powerful way of differentiating between students since the rate at which you increase the amount of autonomy you give a student will depend upon their competence. By starting students off, initially at least, with tasks that address lower levels of attainment in the core skills that they will eventually need will ensure success and motivation, and give the students something to build on.

The range statements

The range statements (Table 6.3) help in making clearer the meaning of phrases like ‘a range of people’ and ‘a range of matters’. However, one of the limitations of criterion-referenced systems of assessment, like the one being used here, is the extent to which you can specify exactly what is meant by certain phrases and words. There is a danger of getting into an infinite regress in an attempt to specify more and more exactly what it is the student has to do. This re-emphasises the need for you to check your understanding of certain phrases with your colleagues and with your external verifier before you start assessing. It will be a bit late to find that your interpretation of a key phrase is different from that of the external verifier at the final moderation visit.

However, a good rule of thumb is ‘does it seem reasonable?’. For example a student working on an assignment which involved interviewing the staff of a company about the work they were doing would be ‘discussing with a range of people’ whilst a student working in a group with other GNVQ students would only be having discussions with ‘known people’.

Table 6.3(a) *Range Statements for the first element of achievement for the mandatory core skill unit* **Communication**

	Level 1	**Level 2**	**Level 3**
Element 1			
Subject matters:	Routine matters (e.g. responding to day-to-day enquiries)	Routine matters (e.g. responding to day-to-day enquiries; discussing routine tasks)	Routine matters (e.g. responding to day-to-day enquiries; discussing routine tasks); complex and non-routine matters (e.g. solving problems, dealing with sensitive issues)
Mode:	Face to face	Face to face; using the telephone	Face to face; using the telephone
Audience:	People familiar with the subject matter and in frequent contact with the individual (e.g. supervisors, colleagues, peers, tutors)	People familiar with the subject matter and in frequent contact with the individual (e.g. supervisors, colleagues, peers, tutors); people familiar with the subject matter but not in frequent contact with the individual (e.g. some customers/clients)	People familiar with the subject matter and in frequent contact with the individual (e.g. supervisors, colleagues, peers, tutors); people familiar with the subject matter but not in frequent contact with the individual (e.g. some customers/clients); people unfamiliar with the subject matter and not in frequent contact with the individual (e.g. some customers/clients, visitors)

Table 6.3(b) *Range statements for the second element of achievement for the mandatory core skill* **Communication**

Element 2	**Level 1**	**Level 2**	**Level 3**
Subject matters:	Routine matters (e.g. day-to-day work processes; breakdowns of machinery; minor incidents)	Routine matters (e.g. day-to-day organisation and administration; responding to customers' letters)	Routine matters (e.g. day-to-day organisation and administration; handling customers' letters); complex and non-routine matters (e.g. a report on a piece of research; a letter on a sensitive issue; summarising a complex document)
Format:	Pre-set format (e.g. record and report cards, memos)	Pre-set format (e.g. record and report cards, memos); outline formats (e.g. letters, reports, log-book entries)	Pre-set format (e.g. record and report cards, memos); outline formats (e.g. letters, reports, log-book entries), freely structured documents (where the structure is determined by the individual)
Conventions:	Use of full stop, comma, capital letters, sentences	Use of full stop, comma, apostrophe, capital letters, sentences and paragraphs	Use of full stop, comma, apostrophe, colon, semi-colon, capital letters, sentences, paragraphs; use of highlighting and indentation to enhance meaning
Audience:	People familiar with the subject matter and in frequent contact with the individual (e.g. supervisors, colleagues, peers, tutors)	People familiar with the subject matter and in frequent contact with the individual (e.g. supervisors, colleagues, peers, tutors); people familiar with the subject matter but not in frequent contact with the individual (e.g. some customers/clients)	People familiar with the subject matter and in frequent contact with the individual (e.g. supervisors, colleagues, peers, tutors); people familiar with the subject matter but not in frequent contact with the individual (e.g. some customers/clients); people unfamiliar with the subject matter and not in frequent contact with the individual (e.g. some customers/clients, visitors)

Table 6.3(c) *Range statements for the* **third element** *of achievement for the mandatory core skill* **Communication**

Element 3	**Level 1**	**Level 2**	**Level 3**
Subject matters:	Routine matters (e.g. day-to-day work processes; breakdowns of machinery; minor incidents)	Routine matters (e.g. day-to-day organisation and administration; responding to customers' letters)	Routine matters (e.g. day-to-day organisation and administration; responding to customers' letters); complex and non-routine matters (e.g. a report on a piece of research; a letter on a sensitive issue)
Images:	Selected from those readily available in the context (e.g. sketches, diagrams, still photographs, charts)	Selected from those readily available in the context; produced to meet a specific need (e.g. sketches, diagrams, still photographs, charts)	Selected from those readily available in the context; produced to meet a specific need (e.g. sketches, diagrams, still photographs, charts)
Audience:	People familiar with the subject matter and in frequent contact with the individual (e.g. supervisors, colleagues, peers, tutors)	People familiar with the subject matter and in frequent contact with the individual (e.g. supervisors, colleagues, peers, tutors); people familiar with the subject matter but not in frequent contact with the individual (e.g. some customers/clients)	People familiar with the subject matter and in frequent contact with the individual (e.g. supervisors, colleagues, peers, tutors); people familiar with the subject matter but not in frequent contact with the individual (e.g. some customers/clients); people unfamiliar with the subject matter and not in frequent contact with the individual (e.g. some customers/clients)

Table 6.3(d) *Range statements for the* **fourth element** *of achievement for the mandatory core skill* **Communication**

Element 4	**Level 1**	**Level 2**	**Level 3**
Subject matters:	Routine matters (e.g. day-to-day work processes; breakdowns of equipment, minor incidents)	Routine matters (e.g. day-to-day organisation and administration; responding to customers' letters)	Routine matters (e.g. day-to-day organisation and administration; responding to customers' letters); complex and non-routine matters (e.g. a report on a piece of research; a letter on a sensitive issue)
Format:	Pre-set format (e.g. record and report cards, memos)	Pre-set format (e.g. record and report cards, memos); outline formats (e.g. letters, reports, log-book entries)	Pre-set format (e.g. record and report cards, memos); outline formats (e.g. letters, reports, log-book entries); freely structured (e.g. wide variety of documents from publicity materials to books and formal reports)
Images:	Used commonly in the context (e.g. sketches, diagrams, still photographs, charts)	Used commonly in the context (e.g. sketches, diagrams, still photographs, charts)	Used commonly in the context (e.g. sketches, diagrams, still photographs, charts); images which have been used by others to illustrate complex/difficult points
Sources of clarification:	Provided for the individual; written (e.g. dictionaries, manuals); oral (e.g. supervisors, tutors, colleagues)	Provided for the individual; written (e.g. dictionaries, manuals); oral (e.g. supervisors, tutors, colleagues)	Provided for the individual; having to be identified and sought out by the individual; written (e.g. dictionaries, manuals); oral (e.g. supervisors, tutors, colleagues)

Implications for teaching

This change in context, from known and familiar settings to unfamiliar ones, can be quite daunting for many students and again hints at appropriate activities and teaching strategies. For example, to achieve some of the higher levels in Element 1 of Communication will require a major boost in the self-confidence of many students. This suggests that exercises which enable students to develop and reflect on their public speaking ability should be part of a core skill development programme in this area.

Students are also likely to require access to staff experienced in developing such skills if they are going to be successful. They may need to be video-taped (which provides evidence of achievement too) so that they can monitor and evaluate their performance and so plan to improve it with your help. It is by using this careful interpretation of the meaning of the elements and their associated performance criteria and range statements, thinking through what students have to do, what underpinning knowledge that might require and tailoring it to the needs of your students, that enables you to come up with the teaching needed for core skill development. Sometimes that is straightforward; often it is not and you will have to think hard and imaginatively.

For example the requirements for punctuation are clear, but how do you teach it? Drilling the students may be a real turn-off but they do need to demonstrate they can punctuate accurately and well. You will need to evolve a strategy which fits with your institution and the needs of your students. This may involve your students in quite explicit learning about the use of punctuation with standard exercises being used to give them practice. The same would be true of spelling too. However, if you can set this in a vocational context, explaining why it is important in the real world, then you are more likely to get a positive response.

Progression and differentiation

The range statements also re-emphasise the need for differentiation and planning for progression in the teaching of core skills. Students are likely to come to you with quite wide differences in terms of their previous achievement in all core skill areas. Their starting-point needs to be identified early on in the course and a plan for their core skill development drawn up. This identification of need in core skill areas can be achieved by reviewing previous work or even by the use of diagnostic testing, though the effects of such a strategy on student self-esteem needs to be watched. You may simply be reinforcing the stereotype they have of themselves. Such tests do, however, constitute valid evidence that the student has covered parts of the range statements.

Beware, also, of thinking that because a student has English Language GCSE at grade C or above (equivalent to Level 3 in the GNVQ core skill levels of attainment; see Table 5.1) they will be able to demonstrate achievement in all of the communication skills specified at Level 3 without further help. The student has to produce evidence of achievement in a practical setting and whilst there is some relationship between the communication core skill unit and the National Curriculum it is not that tight. Certainly they are unlikely to be able to produce evidence of, for example, previous achievement of communicating with the range of audiences in the range of ways needed for GNVQ.

Staffing

The final general lesson to be learnt from study of the communication core skill is about staff responsibility within a GNVQ course team. I can illustrate what I mean by using Element 4 of the Communication unit, which is concerned with the use of images in communication and the performance criteria and range statements for Elements 2 and 3, which emphasise that students are supposed to be writing for a range of audiences using a range of formats. These elements make it clear, I think, that the communication core skills unit is not just about learning more English, though that is important, but about communication in general. The implication, I think, is clear. You cannot simply hand the Communication unit over to an English teacher to be delivered. There are several reasons for this.

Firstly there is a big difference between teaching English and teaching communications which is reflected in the different subject knowledge of teachers of English and of communications, and in their training. Specialist communications teachers, for example, often have a good grasp of the psychological aspects of communication whilst English teachers, where the emphasis in training is often on the teaching of literature, may not. English teachers may, therefore, simply not have all the necessary subject knowledge to teach all of the Communication unit and asking them to do this on their own may be an unreasonable request. You should also beware of falling into the trap of 'Well, we are all teachers of communication so we can do that'. Do you have the necessary understanding of what makes for effective communication to teach it to students?

Secondly English teachers may not understand the nature of the audiences with which the students are expected to communicate, e.g. scientists or business people. The communication skills do need to be developed in context, i.e. not just communicating *per se* but, for those doing, for example, the Art and Design GNVQ, communicating with graphic designers. Those contexts should be familiar to the vocational specialists teaching on a course but they may be very alien to an English teacher who might, therefore, not be able to help much with this aspect of the communications unit. However, the communication units do require the development of general literacy skills, in punctuation, for example, with which an English specialist might be able to help a lot.

Thirdly, to cover some of the range, for example producing documents with different formats which incorporate images, requires teachers with specific skills in the areas of desk top publishing and the use of multimedia. Such skills may be better developed amongst IT teachers rather than English teachers.

Teaching core skills is, therefore, likely to be a multidisciplinary affair involving development and practice of core skill competence in both vocational contexts, e.g. a design studio or an office, and in a general education context, e.g. a literacy or English workshop. This emphasises the need for joint understanding of the core skill units by all the teachers contributing to a programme and joint planning of the programme which depends on good, regular communication between them. In the absence of such communication and planning core skill competence development is likely to be poor.

The dual nature of core skills, their vocational and general education purposes, also raises the issue of transferability: helping students to use skills they have developed in one context in another. This will be a recurring theme throughout the remainder of this section.

6.2 APPLICATION OF NUMBER

Numeracy, or rather the lack of it, is, along with literacy, the core skill which holds the greatest attention in the media. It is important to emphasise therefore that this core skill unit stresses the application of numeracy, not the study and development of mathematical knowledge for its own sake. So, although a knowledge of maths is essential it is not sufficient to demonstrate achievement in the Application of Number core skill unit.

Vocational contexts and learning

It is surprising what students who have formerly struggled with even quite basic numerical concepts can achieve when they are asked to work in a more applied way, especially when they are applying number in a vocational setting:

> I used to be hopeless at maths at school. I just didn't understand it. But I think I'm better now. Seeing what it's for helps you to learn it. (Intermediate Business Studies student)

Another student in the same class who, after assuring me, rather proudly, that she was *'hopeless'* at maths, went and did a fairly complex series of mathematical calculations as part of her work on costing goods and services. When asked why she thought she was not very good at maths, given the calculations she had just done, I got the following reply: 'Oh ... but that's not maths, that's business.'

The worrying thing about this apparently charming answer is that this student did not recognise the mathematical skill she was using. This means that

- she would have difficulty in claiming the core skills she was developing in this area when the assignment she was working on was assessed
- she would have difficulty in reflecting on and improving her core skills in this area
- she would probably have difficulty in applying the skills she had in a new context since she had indexed them so strongly to that assignment and 'doing business', i.e. she might have difficulty in transferring the skills she has learnt.

KEY IDEA: Students need to be made aware of the core skills they are using when working on vocational assignments so that they can practise, reflect on their current performance, and so improve their achievement.

This suggests that opportunities for core skill development and assessment need to be identified on assignment cover sheets and discussed with students when an assignment is first introduced to them. They soon get the hang of this and can then begin to identify the core skill development and assessment opportunities for themselves.

Themes and elements

Three key themes are identified throughout all the Application of Number units:

- gathering and processing data
- representing and tackling problems
- interpreting and presenting data,

and these are developed into the three elements of achievement found in the Application of Number units at the different levels.

The way the elements and performance criteria relate to the levels of the Application of Number core skill unit is shown in Table 6.4. The elements of achievement have an identical structure regardless of the level you are working at. Thus the first element becomes Gather and process data at core skill Level 1; Gather and process data at core skill Level 2; and so on. Enlightenment as to what this actually means comes from inspection of the performance criteria and the range statement (Tables 6.4 and 6.5.)

Performance criteria

The performance criteria associated with each element of achievement are the same for all levels of the application of number unit (Table 6.4). So it is not the generic nature of the performance which is changing as the level increases. Consequently neither the performance criteria nor the elements of achievement are of much use in planning for progression in this unit unlike the Communication unit. Notice also the cross-referencing to Mathematics in the National Curriculum attainment targets and levels in the performance criteria (e.g. AT1 3b = Attainment target 1, Level 3b). This suggests that a copy of the National Curriculum mathematics document will be useful in understanding the performance criteria. Make sure you get a copy of the old attainment targets, the ones in the ring file, rather than the more recent consultation document where levels are not referred to as explicitly.

Range statements

The range statements are the key to understanding this unit and working out what students have to do. These are shown in Table

Table 6.4 *The elements of achievement and performance criteria for the mandatory core skill* **Application of Number**. *Simply replace X in the element statement with 1, 2 or 3 depending on the level of qualification you are working at. The performance criteria are the same at each level for each element hence there is no indication of level given in the table. You should read down and not across the table since alignment of statements across the table is not intended to show their comparability*

Element 1: Gather and process data at core skill level X	Element 2: Represent and tackle problems at core skill level X	Element 3: Interpret and present mathematical data at core skill level X
Techniques appropriate to the task are selected and used by the individual	Techniques appropriate to the task are selected and used by the individual	Trends/significant features of data are identified correctly
Activities required by the techniques are performed to appropriate levels of precision and in the correct sequence	Activities required by the techniques are performed to appropriate levels of precision and in the correct sequence	Conclusions/generalisations/predictions drawn from the data are valid
Mathematical terms and mathematical aspects of everyday language are used and interpreted with precision (AT1 3b)	Mathematical terms and mathematical aspects of everyday language are used and interpreted with precision (AT1 3b)	Clear justification is given for the interpretation of the data
Data are recorded in the required units	Use estimation to check calculations (AT2 4e)	Conventions for presenting data are followed accurately
Data are recorded in the required format	Calculations and results obtained are correct	Data are represented accurately and to appropriate levels of precision
Records are accurate and complete	Aids are used correctly	
	Conclusions/generalisations/predictions drawn from results are valid	
	Clear justification is given for the interpretation of results	

6.5. The format of this table is a little different and requires some explanation. The following conventions are used:

- All range statements in plain typeface, e.g. make estimates based on familiar units of measurement, checking results (AT2 3d) are required for all levels of achievement up to Level 3
- All range statements in italic typeface, e.g. *design and use an observation sheet to collect data (AT5 5b)*, are required for Levels 2 and 3
- Range statements in bold italic face, e.g. ***organise data in groups and classifications***, are required only at Level 3.

Put another way an advanced GNVQ student would be expected to provide evidence of having covered all of the range statements shown in Table 6.5. A foundation GNVQ student would only have to demonstrate coverage of those shown in plain type.

Notice from Table 6.5 how the range increases with level and that each higher level subsumes the lower levels, i.e. the range statements are nested. Notice in particular the large increase in the range in Element 2 as you go from Level 1 to Level 2. This brings in techniques and arithmetical procedures which require more abstract thinking and may, therefore, prove difficult for some students. Given that under most circumstances Intermediate GNVQ students would be expected to complete the qualification in one year, it is clear that they must have some degree of mathematical proficiency before they start. If previous achievement in maths is not good then such students may be better off on a Foundation course, specifically to improve their basic skills, before moving on to Intermediate. Given the draconian financial penalties to FE colleges of enrolling a student for a qualification which is not then achieved, because of, say, a weakness in mathematics which has not been remedied in time, you will realise the need to get students on the right course. Making that decision must take core skills into account.

Subject knowledge

Interpreting the Application of Number units also exemplifies two practical problems for teachers which apply, to some extent, across all GNVQs. Firstly the technical terminology used makes interpretation of the actual meaning of the performance criteria and range statements difficult for teachers without a background in mathematics. Part of the process of getting to know the units must involve

Table 6.5 *Range statements for the mandatory core skill unit* **Application of Number**. *See text for explanation of the conventions governing the use of different forms of text within the table*

Element 1	Element 2	Element 3
Techniques:	**Techniques:**	**Techniques:**
Make estimates based on familiar units of measurement, checking results (AT2 3d)	Solve whole number problems involving addition and subtraction (AT2 2b)	Use mathematical terms to describe common 2D shapes and 3D objects (AT4 2a)
Conduct a survey on an issue of the individual's choice (AT5 4b)	Solve problems involving multiplication and division (AT2 3c)	Construct and interpret statistical diagrams (AT5 3b)
Convert between different units of measurement using tables, graphs and scales	Use fraction, decimals and percentages to describe situations (AT2 4c)	Use the mean and range of a set of data (AT5 4c)
Design and use an observation sheet to collect data (AT5 5b)	Use simple formulae expressed in words (AT3 4b)	Use symbols and diagrams
		Use 2D representation of 3D objects (AT4 6a)
Design and use a questionnaire to survey opinion (AT5 6a)	Find perimeters, areas and volumes (AT4 4d)	*Identify all the outcomes of combining two independent events (AT5 6c)*
Organise data into groups and classifications	*Use networks to solve problems (AT4 5c)*	***Given the probability of exclusive events calculate the probability of a combined event (AT5 7c)***
	Find areas of plane shapes and volumes of simple solids (AT4 5d)	
	Calculate with fractions, decimals, percentages and ratios (AT2 6a)	**Data:** produced by working through activities described in elements X.1 and X.2
	Solve simple equations (AT3 6b)	
	Know and use the formulae for finding the area and circumference of circles (AT4 6d)	
	Use symbolic notation to express the rules of sequence (AT3 7b)	
	Solve equations or simple inequalities (AT4 7d)	

trying to understand what, for example, using 'symbolic notation to express rules of sequences' (Element 2, Level 3) actually means. This suggests that a mathematician, or at least someone with a sound background knowledge of mathematics, needs to be involved as an adviser. The National Curriculum documentation can also help since you are referred to specific attainment targets (ATs) by the range statements and performance criteria.

Secondly since the core skill units are generic, i.e. they apply to all GNVQs, all GNVQ students have to pass all the elements of each core skill unit to gain the GNVQ. This means that they have to provide evidence that they have covered the range. This means that vocational areas where emphasis has not, traditionally, been placed on developing high levels of mathematical proficiency are now required to provide students working at Level 3 to solve equations or carry out calculations in plane and solid shapes. Given the rider above, that core skills need to be developed and applied in vocational settings, this means that you will need to devise assessment tasks for your students which allow them to demonstrate the application of these numeracy skills in the vocational area they have chosen. Again this dilemma emphasises the dual nature of the rationale for GNVQ core skills: developing vocationally relevant achievement in the core skill areas and providing a general educational foundation for further study.

Staffing

The Application of Number unit also raises similar issues to do with staffing GNVQ courses, as was discussed in the previous section on communication. The range statements for the Application of Number unit look more like a conventional syllabus than anything else you will encounter in GNVQ. There is, therefore, a great temptation to hand these over to a mathematician and ask them to get on with it. This temptation is even stronger when, as many GNVQ staff will readily admit, you are not too confident of your own mathematical skills. Again I would argue that this is a mistake, since by devolving responsibility in this way you can easily lose the vocational focus which, as with the two business studies students referred to earlier, gives the mathematics learning a point. Furthermore, your students will have difficulty in generating evidence in the practical **application** of number. This emphasises again the need for team work and also the need for individual members of staff to up-grade their own competence in these core skill areas so that, over time, they can better recognise the opportunities for core skill development and assessment in the work they are doing with GNVQ students.

The final point to be made about the Application of Number units is that they are not easy. Indeed many students have found this unit particularly difficult. It is not just the development of mathematical proficiency that is problematic but the emphasis being placed in the performance criteria on selecting the appropriate technique. This involves extracting the mathematical problem from its setting. Research indicates that many children find this difficult. Your students are, therefore, likely to need considerable help and support with this core skill unit. Ways of providing this are discussed in Chapter 7.

6.3 INFORMATION TECHNOLOGY

Compared with the first two mandatory core skill units, which have been generally welcomed by teachers and employers, this mandatory core skill unit has come in for some criticism. It is not that this skill area is unimportant but the specifications of the units have been described by some as difficult to understand, and demand tasks which IT network managers specifically set out to prevent students from doing, e.g. changing settings and accessing the operating system files. As one network manager put it: 'I try my best to hide those things [the operating system] from the students and the same would be true in an office.'

This has sometimes led to an element of artificiality in the teaching of this core skill and providing evidence of coverage of the range. For example one advanced business studies course set up a specific exercise in which students were allowed to alter settings and collect evidence to show they had covered the range. The system was then crashed, so that all the students' changes were lost, and then rebooted with the original settings.

The ease with which you can carry out some of the operations specified in the range also varies between computing environments, and access to equipment remains a perennial problem. You may have to negotiate for increased access or for more equipment. Do not be afraid to make your case using the connection with demonstrating success in a vocational context. You also need to be aware of how often students can use IT in their day to day work. Could they do some calculations using a spreadsheet or word-process a document using DTP? Look carefully at your vocational assignments and see where the opportunities are once you are familiar with the demands of the IT core skill units.

Themes and elements

Five key themes are identified in the Information Technology units:

- storing and inputting information
- editing and organising information
- presenting information
- evaluating procedures and features of applications
- dealing with errors and faults,

producing five elements of achievement at each level of the qualification (Table 6.6). Analysis of the unit specifications suggests that progression up the levels depends upon students demonstrating:

- an increasing breadth in their use of information technology
- an increasing complexity in the operations they perform.

Performance criteria and range

The above trend is evident from the listing of elements of achievement in Table 6.6 but is seen better by looking at changes in performance criteria and range statements within an element. Table 6.7 lists the performance criteria and Table 6.8 the range statements for the first element of achievement of the Information Technology unit. The convention used previously applies here, evidence of coverage of the range statements in plain type has to be produced by students at all levels, of attainment those in italic by those working at Level 2 and above, those in bold italic at Levels 3 and above.

Notice again the bedding of lower levels within the higher ones so that there is a natural progression in skill development and the underpinning knowledge and understanding. Here the complexity of the requirements laid down in the element statement increases, extra performance criteria are added and the range increases as you move up the levels. Many of the tasks required are not trivial and there will be a need to teach, explicitly, IT skills. Simply sending off a student to word-process a report will not necessarily generate the evidence they require. The development of these skills, as with those specified by the Communication and Application of

Table 6.6 *The five elements of achievement for the mandatory core skill* **Information Technology.** *Systematic changes across the table are highlighted by the use of* ***bold italics***

	Level 1	Level 2	Level 3
Element 1	Input information into specified locations	Set up storage systems and input information	Set system options, set up storage systems and input information
Element 2	Edit and organise information within individual applications	Edit, organise and integrate information from ***different sources***	Edit, organise and integrate ***complex*** information from different sources
Element 3	Present information in pre-set formats	***Select and use formats for presentation***	Select and use formats for presenting ***complex information***
Element 4	Evaluate features and facilities of given applications	Evaluate features and facilities of given applications	Evaluate features and facilities of applications ***already available in the setting***
Element 5	Deal with errors and faults at Level 1	Deal with errors and faults at ***Level 2***	Deal with errors and faults at ***Level 3***

Table 6.7 *Performance criteria for the first element of achievement for the mandatory core skill* **Information Technology.** *Level 1 performance criteria are in* plain type. *Level 2 = Level 1 performance criteria plus those in italics; Level 3 = Level 2 peformance criteria plus those in* ***bold italics***

Information is entered in full and conforms to requirements/conventions regarding labelling, format and place within file(s)/records
Information is entered using a format which will enable any subsequent editing to be carried out efficiently
Copies of drafts/source information are retained as directed
The organisation of storage system allows applications to run efficiently and allows efficient retrieval and transfer of information
Security routines are used to protect information from accidental deletion/disruption and tampering
Changes in systems options result in faster, easier working
Changes in systems options do not interfere adversely with other users' requirements

Table 6.8 *Range statements for the* **first element** *of the mandatory core skill unit* **Information Technology**. *Note that requirements for Level 1 are shown in* plain type. *Level 2 = Level 1 plus range statements in italic; Level 3 = Level 2 plus range statements in* ***bold italics***

Range:	
Type of information:	Textual; graphical; numerical
Type of application:	Those used for storing and presenting textual information; those used for storing and presenting graphical information; those used for storing and presenting numerical information
Storage system:	Existing systems; *new systems established by the individual (e.g. directory systems, folder/file systems)*
Labelling conventions:	Existing; *new conventions established by the individual (e.g. file names, directory names, information tags)*
Type of system options:	***Facilities relating to the working environment (e.g. mouse speed, cursor speed, screen colours); initiating communications between devices (e.g. setting up ports, selecting and loading printer drivers)***

Number units, is not just going to happen. Students have got to learn the IT skills, reflect on their ability in them and plan to improve their levels of achievement in IT.

Again Intermediate students are likely to face the most demanding time in that they have only a year to develop these skills. However, IT requirements of the National Curriculum means that students should come to you with at least some of these skills developed and they should have evidence of their previous achievement which you can use for accreditation of prior learning. None the less, early diagnosis of skills weakness in this area is also needed, with carefully planned and co-ordinated programmes of skill development being implemented for individual students. Again an IT expert would be a useful addition to a course team to act as an adviser and support teacher.

6.4 INTEGRATING THE MANDATORY CORE SKILLS WITH VOCATIONAL UNITS

As discussed in the previous chapter, it is recommended by both NCVQ and the awarding bodies that core skills should be developed and demonstrated as far as possible in the vocational context. The ease with which you can do this does depend on the vocational area, however. It may be that you will have to create a quite artificial situation to allow some students to produce evidence of some core skills. This is partly an artefact of the dual rationale of core skills: on the one hand as part of a general education, on the other as vocationally specific skills needed by employers. None the less it is possible to achieve considerable integration of core skills in all GNVQ areas. Indeed, as one business GNVQ tutor pointed out to me, showing her assignments to a maths expert identified potential for core skill development which she had not spotted.

An example

If we take as an example the following element of achievement from Unit 2, Communicate product design, of the Advanced GNVQ in Manufacturing, you will begin to see how core skills can be mapped on to and integrated with the vocational units.

Element 2.2 Prepare and present design proposals
Performance criteria:

1. aims of presentation are established.

2. presentation methods are selected to match the content of the design proposals and the needs of the audience.
3. information supporting and complementing the presentation is prepared.
4. style and delivery of the presentation are matched to the needs of the audience.
5. presentation demonstrates an ability to communicate effectively.
6. audience are encouraged and given opportunities to ask questions and seek clarification.
7. audience feedback is analysed.

Range: Aims of presentation: for self/peer assessment; for tutor assessment; for customer/client (actual or simulated).

Presentation: formal (e.g. demonstration or explanation leading to negotiated agreement with customer/client); informal (e.g. explanation or information leading to discussion with peers of image conveyed or quality of solution).

Presentation methods: mounting and display techniques; visual presentation systems (OHP, handouts, models, mock-ups); oral presentation systems (e.g. spoken response matched to presented material).

Information: graphical; written.

Audience: known (e.g. peers, tutor/assessor(s)); unknown (e.g. customer/client, simulated or actual).

An approach to mapping

The team teaching this unit had started by sticking the element specification on the left half of an A3 sheet of paper. On the other they began to stick or write down the core skill areas they could cover using this particular element. I would hope after reading this chapter you would see straight away that a lot of the communication unit is covered. Furthermore a student has an opportunity to cover different parts of the range and to produce evidence at different levels. If the assignment you were setting, which incorporated this element, was early on in the course you might expect students to be working on less demanding parts of the range. Later students would be given another opportunity to produce evidence that they were covering more difficult parts of the range of the communication unit after they had more time to develop their communication skills. Remember this is not an all or nothing process. Plan to give your students plenty of opportunities. Furthermore by identifying the core skills which are being developed and which can be assessed in an assignment you are making it obvious to a student what you want them to achieve. The level at which they are going to work can then be negotiated and recorded on the action plan for the assignment. Such planning can also contribute to the overall grading of the portfolio of work too.

If the handouts or OHPs containing both graphical and written material were produced by a computer then there would also be coverage of some of the IT core skill. There is probably no opportunity for development in the application of number core skill but it is a good idea not to put too much into one assignment anyway. If you went through the activity I suggested above with every single one of the vocational units you were teaching identifying the core skills which could be developed and assessed, element by element, then you would end up with a sort of enormous map of core skills linked to vocational elements. The best way I have seen this displayed is on a wall, literally a whole wall, where everyone in the course team can look at it. You now start to look for gaps in coverage, opportunities to practise core skills, times to put in underpinning knowledge, assessment opportunities. This is the first step in a mapping exercise which is considered further in Chapter 7. It can be done, but it takes time and thought.

Chapter 7

Teaching, Learning and Assessing Core Skills

A common feeling about teaching core skills in an integrated way is 'Good idea, but how do I do it?' Indeed you may ask 'Do I have to do it, isn't it someone else's responsibility? After all I only know about finance or physics or design. What part can I play? Anyway I've got enough to do just teaching my bit.' All of these are sentiments I have heard being expressed at the beginning of courses but by the end of a course or at the end of the first year, once people have gained confidence working with the core skill and vocational units, have established patterns of working and find they produce motivated students who want to learn, then they often change their mind.

Sometimes this can go too far, with some vocational teachers wanting to do everything, including all the core skill teaching. Whilst such aspirations are very worthy there is a need for realistic appraisal about what you can achieve and contribute. You may be doing your students a disservice by trying to 'do it all yourself' since you may be denying them access to more expert knowledge and teaching. So I think there are three messages which need to come out of this chapter:

- You learn about teaching and assessing core skills by doing it. This gives you confidence but takes time, may require your own personal development through in-service activities and the need to rethink your approach to teaching, at least a bit
- Students learn about core skills by engaging in programmes which take core skill development seriously, which make the core skills they are developing obvious and which exploit every opportunity for assessing core skills
- Both of the above depend on team work, good communications and advanced planning. Whilst setting this up may be primarily a management operation it does demand that all the staff involved are prepared to work in a team, share their ideas and take responsibility for new areas of work. This is also likely to require a commitment to personal development.

The element of experience and developing solutions which fit the needs of your institution and your students are just as important then for teaching and assessing the core skill units as they are for the vocational units. No book can tell you how to teach – you must decide that for yourself. What this chapter can do however is to make you aware of what the awarding bodies and NCVQ expect, how those expectations might be translated into action and how others have gone about implementing core skill programmes.

7.1 ESSENTIAL RESOURCES

You need to equip yourself with some key documents. In addition to the centre guidelines from the awarding bodies (it is worth acquiring all of them, especially the one from BTEC) you should obtain a copy of the NCVQ (1993b) document, assessing core skills in GNVQs and the exemplar assessment material being produced by NCVQ for each GNVQ area since this also includes material which shows how to assess core skills. Finally there is some worthwhile material produced by FEU, especially the core skills action pack. Rather than reproducing this vast amount of material here I shall try to draw out some general principles for teaching, learning and assessing core skills.

Time

Before you can even begin to think about a strategy for delivering the core skills you do need to be thoroughly familiar with both the vocational skill units in your area and the core skill units. This is a tall order and is unlikely to happen overnight. It will require some degree of commitment and ideally some time set aside for meetings both for familiarisation and developing the programme. The extent to which you can achieve this goal will of course depend upon your institution. But one of the purposes of writing this book was to enable you to argue for time and resources with your senior management, by providing you with a detailed understanding of GNVQ and its resource requirements. If you have worked your way through the book to this point you probably now have a better understanding of the demands and requirements of GNVQ than the senior managers. Combining this knowledge about GNVQ with arguments based around standards of achievement (e.g. league tables) and funding (e.g. FEFC requirements) you can make a strong case for at least some time. It is worth trying and it does work.

Course teams

You will need expert core skill teachers to help with both designing and teaching programmes for GNVQ core skills. Using such experts will increase confidence that you are getting it right, enrich your assignments and spread the teaching and marking load. The key thing is to get the right people. The red hot A level maths teacher may not be the best person for teaching Application of Number but special needs maths teachers, because they are used to working in different ways with students and responding to different demands, may be. Core skill specialists also have to be committed to working in new ways and within new structures. This may require them to come out of their own subject departments and to teach in laboratories, engineering shops or simulated offices. Clearly they will need time to understand and adapt to GNVQ.

7.2 BUILDING A PROGRAMME

This is much more difficult than either NCVQ or the awarding bodies imply it is. There do seem to be two approaches though.

The strategic approach

This strategy can best be summarised by the following advice from BTEC about developing a strategy for core skill implementation:

> The exercise is best carried out as a team approach. BTEC pilot centres have found the following stages of development helpful:
>
> - consider each Core Skills Unit separately
> - discuss the elements and range statements to reach a shared understanding and interpretation
> - focus on any range statements which cause difficulty for members of the team
> - draw up an implementation plan identifying opportunities for learning and the most appropriate context for assessing
> - map the assessment outcomes against the performance criteria and range statements in the core skill specifications to check coverage
> - map core skills against a programme assessment map (BTEC (1993a) p60)

This is good advice and is echoed by NCVQ and the other awarding bodies but it does need some clarification. Hopefully the previous chapter has helped with getting you started on the first three points in the above list. However, the second three points do have a slight element of jargon about them. What they are suggesting is that having decided what the core skill units mean, do the following:

1. Look at the bank of assignments, tasks, projects etc. you have developed for teaching the vocational skills units and see how the core skill specifications articulate with that work. This is the process of identifying opportunities for learning core skills and providing a context for their assessment. You might also add to your bank of activities to provide additional opportunities. One way of doing this is to let core skill specialists look at the assignments. They may spot opportunities for core skill development that you do not. Alternatively they may suggest alterations to your vocational assignments which would allow students the opportunity to produce evidence of more core achievement than was possible in the original assignment.
2. Take the predicted outcomes of the work you are asking the students to do in these assignments, tasks, projects and so on and identify precisely the match between these outcomes and the performance criteria and range statements in the core skills units. You may be surprised at how much one assignment can deliver. For example in the exemplar materials provided by NCVQ for assessing student's work in business there is an assignment for intermediate students which requires them to compare employment prospects in two areas, organise two work visits and one work placement. The structure of the assignment is such that in addition to covering vocational areas it is also providing an opportunity for students to demonstrate core skill development in all six core skill areas at Level 2.
3. Providing you can identify assessment opportunities a priori these can then be mapped on to some overall programme assessment map, often in the form of a gigantic wall display. Once you have done this for your course, a mammoth task I know, you will then be able to identify any gaps in your provision for core skill development and assessment. You can then make good these deficiencies by providing extra tasks either within existing assignments or by adding new ones.
4. Having identified which assignments, tasks, projects, etc. which will provide the vehicle for delivering the core skills these can then be identified formally on the cover sheet of the assignment

and discussed with the students when the assignment is set. The students can then claim the core skills when they hand in the assignment and you can corroborate their claim by looking at the evidence they have produced. Students can also identify, with help from personal tutors during review sessions (see Theme 3) and teachers when completing assessment action plans, where they may need specific extra help with core skills in order to complete assignments. This help can then be provided, for example, by access to workshop facilities.

KEY IDEA: Vocational activities need to be designed to provide opportunities for students to learn about, practise and demonstrate their core skills.

The reality is, of course, likely to be much more haphazard than this especially at the beginning of a course. The time available and level of experience amongst staff to achieve this degree of forward planning, is likely to be insufficient to complete this enormous task and should you have the whole of a course decided before you start anyway? Where is the opportunity for negotiation with the student? Further, if you are just starting at an institution you are unlikely to have a bank of assignments to work with and you will quite rightly devote your energies to that in the first instance.

The ad hoc approach

This second, more opportunistic strategy, for identifying core skill achievement is based around assessing core skill attainment a posteriori, i.e. you identify what core skills have been achieved after the assignment has been completed. This more haphazard approach is almost inevitable in the early stages of developing a course. However, as your knowledge of and confidence with GNVQ develops you will probably begin moving towards the first model. There should always be an element of the second model though, even when you have a fully mature course, since students may well demonstrate core skills within an assignment which you had not predicted. Alternatively students may produce evidence of core skill achievement through prior achievement which can be accredited (APL) or from non classroom based activities, e.g. work experience, a part-time job or community work. Providing students produce the evidence and providing the assessor is satisfied the evidence is genuine and it meets the performance criteria then why should students not be credited with their achievements? This is especially true when students perform at a level above that which you were expecting.

Another important and I think neglected strategy consists of setting core skill assignments or specific core skill tasks. As I emphasised in the two previous chapters there is knowledge and understanding underpinning performance in these core skill areas. Many students need to be formally taught communications skills, the best way to use an overhead projector, how to use a specific application on a computer, how to calculate percentages, about team work and so on. This can be done through activities designed specifically to do this. Providing students are then asked to use the skill in a vocational setting almost immediately, so that they see the point, or, even better, if the activity comes out of a vocational assignment, i.e. you need to be able to do this to complete this assignment and here's how to learn about it, then they will see the point of the exercise. Indeed making core skills explicit in this way is the most effective way of getting students to reflect on and develop their core skill competence whilst helping them to transfer that competence from one vocational setting to another.

Additional support

The core skill units are not easy and many students will need additional support developing the underpinning knowledge and understanding. Often this support needs to be given on an individual basis. The use of learning support workshops is one way of providing this and they are becoming increasingly common in FE and tertiary colleges. Access to these learning support workshops needs to be negotiated with the students so that they realise the point of their going to the workshop and do not suffer the shock to their self-esteem which can come from being labelled as being in need of additional support. It is also important that the students quickly make use of their new knowledge and/or skills developed in the workshop in a vocational setting.

If you do not have access to such workshops then you need to devise a learning support system for your students. This is especially true in schools who are just starting GNVQ and may, for example, have only one group of students. The resources are simply not going to be available to set up workshops for just this one group. There is no easy solution to this problem.

7.3 TRANSFERABILITY

Have you ever had the following experience? You think about collecting something from upstairs, go upstairs to get it and then promptly forget what it was you were going to collect. When you go downstairs again you remember what it was you had meant to collect. This common, trivial but annoying example illustrates the problem of transferability. We develop our thinking and our skills, including core skills, within a context, and it can remain indexed to that context. Very often when we move to a new context we transfer neither the thinking, e.g. what we were going upstairs to collect, nor the skill.

The latter point can be illustrated further by the use of an anecdote. As a FE college lecturer I was often puzzled by the fact that a group of biology A level students whom I was teaching were unable to do quite simple mathematical work even though they all did A level maths or had good GCSEs in maths. I set up an 'experiment' where the A level maths students in the group were taught about graphical representation in the maths lesson the morning before my biology lesson in the afternoon. In the biology lesson they were asked to analyse some data which required them to use the techniques they had been taught about in maths that morning. The A level maths students did no better on this task than the other students. When we discussed this the reasons soon became clear: this was biology and that was maths. They associated maths with a particular room, teacher and style of working, i.e. a particular context, and biology with me, my lab and my style of working. They had simply not transferred their maths learning: indeed they had not even thought that it was legitimate to do so. Once they were aware of the skills they were developing in maths and I made it clear how they could use them in biology they got a lot better at biological mathematics.

KEY IDEA: Transferability depends, in part, on students being aware of the core skills they are developing and using.

Bridging

Whilst I would not wish to read too much in to my limited experiment it is apparent from other research in this area that students do have problems transferring skills, knowledge and understanding developed in one context into another. Helping them to do this involves building bridges between contexts and this seems to depend upon:

- making the skills they are learning in a particular context obvious to them and giving them high status
- getting them to practise the skills in different contexts so that they realise that the skills can be transferred
- assessing the skills in different contexts, i.e. assess them on a particular core skill more than once
- make the whole process explicit through discussion with the students.

This, I know, adds yet another layer to mapping core skills on to a programme of activities, since you have to identify opportunities for practice and several opportunities for assessment in different vocational contexts. Again you are unlikely to reach this level of sophistication in your planning when you first start, but given the benefits your students, you and your institution will derive from good levels of core skill development it is worth striving for.

The status of core skills

There is some evidence to suggest when core skills are not afforded high status by, for example emphasising them in the assessment specification on the assignment cover sheet or discussing them at length when setting an assignment, that students simply do not bother with them. For example science students when asked what skills they were developing as part of their programme, which contained core skills, couched their answers almost exclusively in terms of science practical skills. A group of GNVQ business study students when asked about core skills they were doing considered them to be irrelevant and that they were only interested 'in doing things which relate directly to business, like finance'.

In neither case did these students take core skills seriously and this was seriously impeding their development in these areas. Discussion with their lecturers suggested that the reason for this is that the lecturers in the vocational subjects did not take them seriously, not because they did not think they were important but because they felt rushed in delivering their part of the programme, thought someone else was 'doing core skills' or did not understand the core skills.

I think the message is clear. If you do not take the core skills seriously and emphasise them through the vocational programme then your students will not take them seriously or value developing their competence in the core skill areas either. Clearly to help students take the core skills on board as an important part of the GNVQ course they need to be exposed to the core skill unit specifications early on. According to research done by NCVQ the key thing to help this happen is ensuring that the lecturers are confident about the core skill units, i.e. they are familiar with the specifications and how they relate to the work in the vocational units. Once again we are back to meeting and talking with your colleagues and bullying senior management into giving you the time to do this.

Talking about core skills needs to take place between you and the students too. This can take the form of:

- whole group discussions about the opportunity a particular assignment offers for core skill development
- discussions with individuals about how their work is progressing
- tutorial sessions specifically designed to discuss specific core skills and setting targets for their development
- identifying opportunities in forthcoming assignments for developing and producing evidence of achievement in core skills.

Try and keep the core skill pot boiling all the time with your students but do this in a co-ordinated way with your colleagues so you all know what the others are doing and how the programme fits together overall. Again this is an ideal situation, a long-term aim, but evidence from America, e.g. from Alverno College in Milwaukee, suggests it really can happen. The keys seem to be ensuring that all members of a course team:

- appreciate the rationale and importance of core skills in GNVQ programmes
- come to a common understanding of the meaning of the core skill units
- develop a team approach to core skill delivery
- map core skills on to the vocational assignments
- develop an efficient tracking system for monitoring core skill development and achievement.

7.4 ASSESSING CORE SKILLS

Assessment of core skills basically follows the same pattern as assessment of the vocational units (Figure 3.1). GNVQ programmes, where core skill development is proceeding smoothly, are characterised by assessment regimes within which core skill achievement is being continually assessed. Whilst there is a range of ways this can be achieved all these programmes seem to have the following characteristics:

- advanced planning of core skill assessment
- identification of core skills to be assessed on assignment cover sheets
- using a range of assessment techniques
- judging evidence validly
- rapid feedback to students on their achievements with a concomitant identification of core skill development needs
- simple recording systems for core skill achievement
- planned progression
- some use being made of APL.

Advance planning

Just as the efficient management of the assessment of the vocational units can best be achieved through the use of assessment plans the same is true of assessing the core skill units. Such a plan, which maps the core skills on a unit by unit basis to different parts of the learning programme, will identify the opportunities for assessing core skills throughout a learning programme on an assignment by assignment basis. They clarify roles, who does what and when, but producing them is an enormous job: 'We now have an assessment plan for the whole of our course but it has taken 18 months to produce it' (Business studies teacher).

They can also become a strait-jacket which is insensitive to the needs of individual students. Thus in the best schemes these course assessment plans are augmented by detailed individual assessment plans for each student drawn up during review sessions, but you do need both.

Identification of core skills in assignments

Once they have been mapped on to assignments core skill development possibilities have to be identified to students. The simplest way to do this is to list them on the assignment cover sheet. They should then be drawn to the attention of the students who should incorporate them into their action plan for covering the work in the assignment.

Using a range of assessment approaches

NCVQ identify three different approaches to assessment which when combined produce the most effective assessment regimes:

- **assessment planning** – both whole course and individual
- **retrospective assessment** – through assessment of outcomes, e.g. reports, artefacts and so on
- **ongoing assessment** – through questioning and observation whilst students are carrying out an activity.

Once the work has been completed and handed in it can then be assessed for core skills achievement. This can involve assessing for core skills achieved which you have identified on the assessment plan and other core skills which the students have provided evidence for, **retrospective assessment**. (Once they are used to using the units specifications students become quite good at spotting their own achievements.)

However, both assessment planning and retrospective assessment are insensitive to evidence which is being produced as students actually do a task. The third technique, **ongoing assessment** picks up this unexpected achievement. It is recording evidence of achievement as somebody is actually doing something, e.g. selecting a particular numerical technique, and is therefore a much more valid form of assessment than asking someone, perhaps weeks later, how they came to do something which they have written about in an assignment. It is particularly useful in the communications unit when you can observe students giving talks and use a tick list to record what they have done. This tick list can then become part of their portfolio of evidence.

The problem is of course finding the time to do the observation and then recording the evidence which, by its very nature, is going to be ephemeral. You also have to remember a lot of detail about the three mandatory core skill units if your assessment is going to use the performance criteria and the range. This comes with experience: both recognising where ongoing assessment is going to be useful and remembering the specifications of standards in the core skill units.

Judging the evidence

The rules for ensuring validity of evidence in the assessment of core skills are the same as those identified for the vocational units (see pp 52–56). However, one common mistake made when assessing core skills is to forget to use the performance criteria to judge the evidence. Rather assessment is based on the assessor recognising that students have completed activities which match a particular element and so thinking that since the student has completed the activity successfully then they must have passed the element.

The NCVQ give a nice example:

> ... Communication 3.1: 'Take part in discussions with a range of people on a range of matters – and then sees [i.e. the assessor sees] which part of the range the activity matches. However, the assessor does not use the performance criteria to judge whether the student has completed the activity successfully. In Communication 3.1 it is very easy to leave out assessment of whether 'own understanding of points made by others is checked and confirmed'. (NCVQ (1993b) p22).

This is an obvious candidate for ongoing assessment. The problem seems to arise through unfamiliarity with the core skill units and a lack of understanding of the detailed nature of GNVQ assessment procedures.

KEY IDEA: Use the performance criteria to decide whether students have successfully completed the activity described in the element and in the settings listed in the range.

Other problems can arise when assessors think that they can tick off the performance criteria for an element in an almost mechanical fashion. Whilst the range can be covered in this piecemeal way the performance criteria cannot. For example, Communication 3.3 requires students to 'Use images to illustrate points made in writing and in discussions with a range of people on a range of matters'. On one occasion students may demonstrate achievement on one part of the associated range statement, say using images to illustrate routine matters on another they might cover another, e.g. illustrating complex and non-routine matters. Tackling the range in this way is all right, if a bit time consuming. However, with very rare exceptions, on each occasion the student's evidence must satisfy all of the performance criteria associated with the element.

KEY IDEA: Performance criteria cannot be bitten off one by one. They all have to be satisfied together for a student to have successfully achieved the activity described in the element.

One final thing to beware of. Just because candidates do not satisfy the standards at one level does not automatically mean they have satisfied the standards at a lower level. You must assess using the performance criteria at the lower level. However, students can be given credit for working at a lower level and early on in a programme that can be quite motivating, since the students feel they are achieving something. For those students who do not reach the level required for the award they are working towards may also be credited with core skills at lower level providing their portfolio contains appropriate and valid evidence of achievement in core skills at that level. At least the student then leaves with something.

Feedback

It is essential that students think about their core skill achievements and so identify areas where further development is needed. The best way to do this is to provide them with feedback on their assignment which makes explicit use of the core skill unit specifications. Problems can then be spotted early. For example, one student who was having problems in achieving 'Communication 2.2 Prepare written material on routine matters' was aware that her problems revolved around an inadequate understanding of the rules of punctuation because she was being told so in the feedback she was getting on her assignments. After three assignments this pattern was picked up by the course tutor from the assignment cover sheets where it was being noted, and the student was guided towards the college literacy workshop for extra support in this area of core skills. She saw the point of the help because she realised what she had to do in order to pass the element.

KEY IDEA: Using the assessment criteria to provide feedback helps students to identify what they are not achieving and helps tutors guide them to additional support.

Record keeping

It is important to keep track of how students are getting on with core skills but at the same time the process can become a bureaucratic nightmare. Keep the tracking paper to a minimum and make extensive use of assignment cover sheets to record achievement. The other tactic to reduce the load on you is to give the students much more responsibility. Once students know how GNVQ works, and that means good induction, (see Theme 3) they will come to you with evidence of their achievement. After all they are the only people who know what they are doing in all the various learning contexts they encounter both in and out of college. Students can also be taught to maintain their own portfolios and complete tracking documentation, which can also count towards core skill achievement. As NCVQ point out, this sort of approach, where you trust students more and more, produces '... benefits in:

- motivating students
- making them more active participants in the assessment process
- reducing the burden on teachers for gathering evidence
- getting students to work directly with the core skill units' (NCVQ (1993b) p13).

Of course you will get slackers but it is easier to chase the few than to chase the many.

Progression

Good assessment plans provide for progression. Thus early on in the course students work on those parts of the range which are easier to deal with, moving on to more difficult aspects later on. For example, early on in the course students could be dealing with those parts of the range from the communication element 3.4 'Read and respond to written materials and images on a range of matters' which deal with using pre-set formats, moving on to freely structured formats later in the course.

KEY IDEA: Early on in the course incorporate assessment opportunities in core skills which are easy to achieve and so enable the student to succeed.

Accreditation of prior learning (APL)

This can be useful for covering the range in some core skill units but must be based on valid and reliable evidence. This could include work done for GCSEs, evidence from a part-time job or from community work. One college instigated an APL week where students had the opportunity, once they had understood how GNVQ worked, to present evidence of prior achievement. It was remarkably successful.

Core skills are important to students: they are the skills they need for life-long learning. Providing they are taught well the core skills they develop during GNVQs are likely to prove more durable than the knowledge they acquire in the vocational units, which will date rapidly.

Theme 3:

The Management of Student Learning

The final set of constraints which need to be taken into account when devising learning programmes for GNVQ are the students themselves. Passing GNVQs and achieving a good grade requires students to be actively involved in their learning. In particular they have to play a more leading role in planning, organising and evaluating their work than they may be used to. GNVQ students not only seem to do well on such an educational diet, they actually like the process:

> 'Its really hard work 'cause you're expected to do so much yourself but I like that.'
>
> 'You never have time to get bored. There's always plenty to do but you can go at your own pace, not writing notes all the time.'
>
> 'I'm getting a good impression. I kind of like it, yeah. You get to work more on your own and do work experience so you can see the sort of jobs you could do.' (Intermediate GNVQ Health and Social Care students)

Furthermore, because they are more involved in planning, organising and evaluating their work, GNVQ students feel more of a sense of responsibility for their own learning which leads, sometimes for the first time in their education, to a real feeling of success:

> 'You're treated different here to school. More involved like. They talk with you and make you think "I've got to do this for myself". That's what I've found out about this course, it's made me aware that I've got to do it for my own good. It's nobody else. It's just for me and if I don't get it done that's it ... but you feel really good when you've done it.' (Advanced Business GNVQ student)

Such feelings of success produce well-motivated students and much of that motivation seems to stem from the different ways of teaching and learning these students are experiencing, combined with the more vocational focus of the work they are doing: many of them emphasise learning about the real world as one of the attractions of doing GNVQ.

All these aspects of GNVQ courses were emphasised at a sixth form conference in 1993 when GNVQ students were reported as stating that 'A levels were not practical enough'; that they wanted more active forms of learning and opportunities to take responsibility for their own learning; that with GNVQ 'what you see is what you get'. (*Education*, 20.11.93)

However, employing active learning strategies, and giving students responsibility for their own learning, does involve developing a different relationship between teacher and learner at the centre of which lies joint management of the student's learning. The complex processes involved in managing student learning form the background to this section of the book which covers:

- A model for managing student learning
- Enrolment and Counselling
- Induction
- Action planning

Throughout, the issues raised are exemplified by the use of case studies, comments from teachers and students. Again these are not intended to show how GNVQ courses should be 'delivered' since they are strategies which have developed in quite different institutions to meet the specific needs of teachers and students working within those institutions. Rather they are intended to illustrate the sort of thinking which has gone into designing systems of managing student learning: thinking which you need to take account of as you come to grips with GNVQ.

Chapter 8

Managing Student Learning: Models and Systems

The active management of student learning, which the GNVQ curriculum model implies, involves the development of close relationships between teachers and students plus record-keeping systems which monitor student progress. Both of these require the development of sophisticated systems if you are not to be overwhelmed by the complexity of the task and the tracking of student achievement. This chapter examines a management of learning model proposed by the Further Education Unit (FEU) (1993b) which seems germane to GNVQ, the implications of that model and three examples of how different course teams have developed their own management systems. Looking at the model shown in Figure 4.1 will also be useful.

8.1 THE FEU MODEL

Managing the learning of a group of students is likely to be a daunting task. To help think through the issues involved, and to suggest some possible mechanisms involved in helping students to manage their learning throughout a course, a model is useful. This is shown in Figure 8.1. This model really is designed to help you think and is not intended to be something which you can apply mechanically in your own institution. As the case studies discussed below show, institutions produce different models which they put into practice. However, all of the case studies do have features which the general model in Figure 8.1 shows. Consequently this is a useful start since it will help you to identify essential features of any model of managing student learning – essential features which you should be trying to put into place.

Course teams are essential

The model assumes that you will be working as part of a course team and that one or more members of the team have been designated

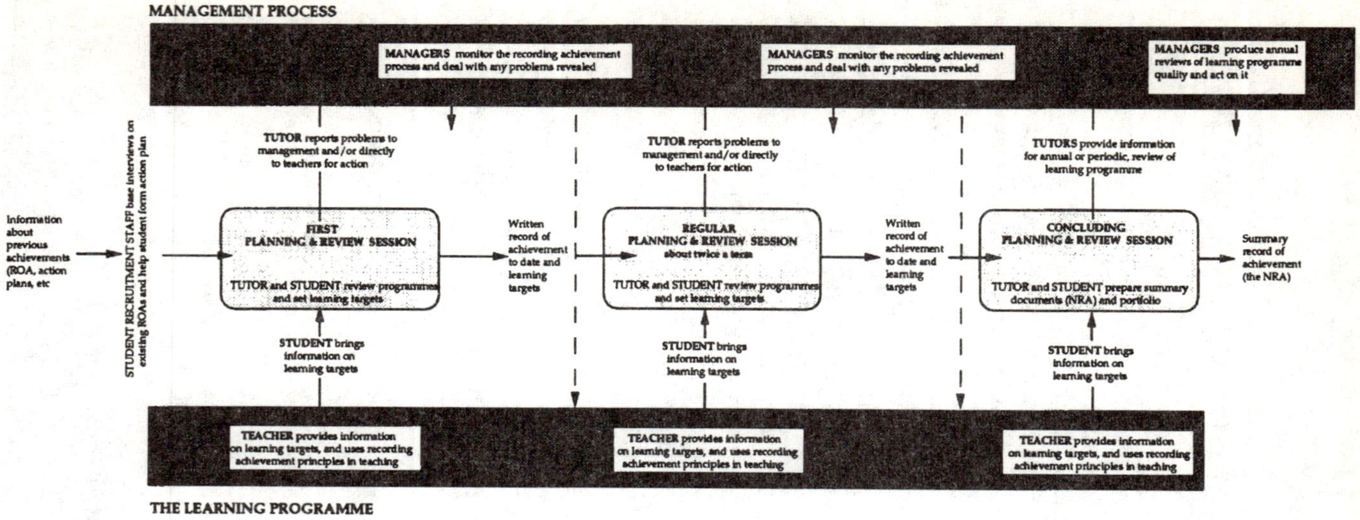

Figure 8.1 *A suggested model for managing the learning of students on programmes like GNVQ. The model is intended to show how students can become more responsible for managing their own learning. (From* Managing Learning, *Further Education Unit 1993.)*

as personal tutors. The personal tutor will be responsible for the processes which occur in the middle of the diagram, the planning and review sessions. Details of what goes into such sessions are given later. The model shows that information is fed to the personal tutor by teaching staff and that this information forms the basis of discussions which occur between the personal tutor and the individual student in a review session. Again mechanisms to support the flow of information from teacher to personal tutor are discussed later. The model also emphasises that everyone, personal tutors, teachers, course managers and, of course, students are essential to the review process. You really do need to work as a team to make this work and you will therefore need to identify ways in which you could do this in your institution as a matter of priority.

Review

The central process in the model is that of review. There are two written outcomes of a review session:

- students produce a written record of achievement, documenting what they have achieved so far. The fact that the student is producing the written report will relieve the tutor of administrative work but can also contribute to the overall grading of a student's portfolio since it constitutes evidence of a student evaluating their own work
- students produce a forward action plan which details what they will be trying to achieve before the next review session. The contents of this action plan should then be communicated to and negotiated with the teachers by students. Again the action plan can contribute to the overall grading of a student's portfolio of work since it constitutes evidence of planning.

KEY IDEA: The process of review involves both looking back to evaluate what the student has a achieved and looking forward to plan what the student is going to try to achieve before the next review.

In addition the review session can lead to information being passed to course managers. This may simply be to let them know that things are going well but it may also be to communicate problems that are occurring. This information allows records to be up-dated and forms the basis on which the overall quality of a course can be monitored. Any problems revealed by the review sessions can then be discussed at course team meetings.

The role of the teacher

It is tempting to think that since you are not a personal tutor you are not really involved in the review process. As Figure 8.1 suggests this is not the case. For example you will have to provide information about learning targets that you expect the student to achieve in the next few weeks, you will need to report successes and problems, the students will be taking along work you have marked and graded to the review session and you will receive feedback from the review session. Teachers are therefore far from sleeping partners in the review process. Indeed they are in fact the beginning and end of the process and are, therefore, essential to its success.

KEY IDEA: All members of a course team are involved in managing student learning.

8.2 THE PERSONAL TUTOR

Clearly the personal tutor plays a central role in the whole process of managing student learning. Furthermore the role is more than just the traditional pastoral one associated with personal tutors. They have to be much more involved in the day to day learning of the student as well as offering pastoral guidance and counselling. For this reason it is essential for the personal tutor to be a member of the course team and a vocational expert since they will need to understand the learning targets being negotiated with students by other vocational teachers.

The personal tutor is sometimes also the course tutor – the person responsible for the day to day management of the course. It needs to be questioned whether this is a good idea on two grounds:

- the workload involved in combining both jobs is enormous
- students need an independent arbiter if things are going wrong. If personal tutors are also overall course managers this places them in a difficult position since they may feel defensive about courses which they have largely defined and they may therefore be reluctant about taking on board genuine and reasonable complaints from students.

Personal tutors to do their job effectively need, therefore, to be very tactful in their dealings with both students and colleagues. In addition the personal tutor does need to carry some clout and this suggests that the person asked to do the job should be an experienced and perhaps senior member of the course team.

Personal tutors also need to develop a special relationship with their students. In particular the FEU emphasise the following qualities:

- the ability to establish a friendly, helpful , purposeful ethos
- be receptive to the student's concerns
- listen sympathetically
- offer sound, practical advice.

The practical implications of all of these statements will be dealt with later in the case studies but one general point worth making here is that the students themselves have to be made aware of the importance and worth of the review sessions. This can best be achieved by ensuring that the students are given a sense of purpose about the review and encouraged to talk about issues important to them. As one tutor put it:

> To begin with I seemed to spend all my time [tutorial time] doing routine paperwork in the review sessions and their students saw them simply as box ticking sessions. The time seemed to go so fast that there was never enough time to talk about anything substantial. I think this is why the students did not really value the sessions and also why other members of the course team began to see them as a waste of time. I had not thought through what their purpose was and my confusion made everyone else confused. (GNVQ personal tutor)

This comment emphasises two further points:

- the course team must agree on the purpose and aims of the review sessions and support each other in its implementation
- the personal tutor needs to be an effective time manager so that the routine tasks are accomplished quickly at the beginning of the review session, leaving the bulk of the time available for discussion.

How you achieve this depends on the way your course is managed but the tutor who was talking about his initial failure above commented:

> I now realise I was doing too much of the paperwork. I felt I needed to control everything. I have now asked my colleagues to share the burden and we have given a lot of responsibility to the students. I now have time to talk with the students about their progress and the sessions are working much better.

This issue of the amount of paperwork involved in running GNVQ courses is a constant one. There is no simple solution but paperwork is essential. Giving the students responsibility reduces the amount of time tutors have to devote to it. New computerised systems which are starting to come on to the market are also going to be important. However, you will always have to face the problem of what happens if students do not exercise the responsibility given to them, i.e. they do not maintain their course folders or fill in the forms correctly. Perhaps rather than worrying you should ask whether such students should gain the qualification anyway. Certainly they do not seem to be exercising many of the core skills, even at the lowest levels, discussed in Theme 2 of this book. They will however need to be taught how to manage their time, work and learning. Review sessions play a key role in this learning process.

KEY IDEA: Time invested in helping students acquire the skills of managing their own learning and portfolios early in the course will reduce the amount of time tutors have to spend on routine paperwork.

8.3 RUNNING REVIEW SESSIONS

If the review sessions are going to be successful it is essential that they are carried out on a one to one basis which immediately raises the question of time. The way in which review sessions are planned varies between institutions but the general consensus seems to be that half an hour is the shortest time in which review meetings can be held. In many cases they last longer, especially at the beginning and end of the course. However, if the time is used to help students really understand what they are trying to achieve then it is not wasted. Indeed one course tutor from a science pilot centre had the following advice for anyone starting the course:

> Think about the amount of time you have available for tutorials and then double it. This is the most important thing that happens with our students.

The environment also has to be right if reviews are going to be successful. Attempting, as I have seen, to conduct a review in the middle of a busy classroom with so much demanding the attention of the teacher is a waste of time and quite frustrating for both tutor and student. Review meetings really do need to take place in a quiet room free from interruptions, e.g. telephone calls.

8.4 CASE STUDIES

To complete this chapter I would like to present three case studies which show how three different institutions approached the implementation of a review process. In all three cases the process was working, up to a point, but each model was presenting different problems. We will come back to these cases as we discuss parts of the review process, induction, on-course review and final review in subsequent chapters. The purpose here is just to give you an overall feel of the process in three different institutions.

Case Study 1

This is a school which has been running GNVQs at intermediate level for one year. The intermediate groups, one in Leisure and Tourism the other in Business, have just one class teacher who also serves as the personal tutor. Neither teacher had previous experience of teaching on vocational courses. There is no formal timetabling of review sessions. Rather the students are given one hour of 'tutorial time' each week but they join in with A level tutorial groups at this time. The reasoning behind this is to create a cohesive atmosphere within the sixth form. However, the tutorial time is used primarily for administrative purposes and as an opportunity to talk about 'things in general'.

The GNVQ induction process had been very short, only two days, and had been largely concerned with administrative matters. This had led to initial problems since the students had not had a clear idea of what they were supposed to be doing and certainly had not come to grips with the language of GNVQ. As a result both teachers decided to run a further induction programme after the first half term. This lasted two weeks and concentrated on helping the students to understand the language of GNVQ.

On-course review differs in the two subjects. The teacher of intermediate GNVQ in Leisure and Tourism has responded to the lack of timetabled review time by using her subject teaching time to provide reviews. However, this means conducting reviews in the classroom where her students are working and the environment is not particularly conducive to the sort of talking needed.

The other teacher is using lunch times for reviews at half-termly intervals. Whilst this is enabling her to talk to students individually and in quiet surroundings it is very draining. Consequently she is beginning to feel that she cannot keep up the review process.

By dint of sheer hard work both these teachers are providing their students with feedback. Both value the detailed knowledge they have of their students because they are the only people who teach them but they also recognise the strains that this places on them in having to teach across the whole of a GNVQ and the vast amount of preparation this has involved. Furthermore whilst they thought initially that combining the role of personal tutor with that of exclusive classroom teacher would make their task easier they now realise that is not the case. In particular they were concerned that students were unwilling to talk about issues to do with the course for fear of offending them.

Clearly this is a system that is being maintained by the professionalism of the staff involved, but the process, whilst it is working, is placing enormous strain on the two individuals involved. This has been realised by senior managers who are timetabling two members of staff to each course for next year with one of them taking on the role of personal tutor and the other that of course manager.

Case Study 2

This FE college has run successful BTEC National and First Diploma programmes in a number of areas and this is reflected in the organisation of the review process. The courses are run by course teams which meet every fortnight for an hour to discuss progress and problems. Each course team has a course tutor who manages the overall running of the course, and a personal tutor.

The induction period lasts three weeks, with specific induction activities planned on a subject by subject basis. For example the Art and Design GNVQ uses induction assignments. These are discussed in more detail in the next chapter. The aim is to ensure that students understand the language of GNVQ and they appreciate the way in which they are going to learn on the course. In particular the course team wants the students to realise that they own the course and that they should not expect to be spoon-fed with information.

The on-course review process is formally timetabled. The normal timetable is suspended every half term for two weeks and course teams are then required to organise their own review procedures. In the case of Art and Design and Leisure and Tourism this takes the form of one week spent in discussion with their classroom teachers and personal tutor. Workshop or studio tasks are negotiated with the students and these are completed when the students are not involved in formal review sessions. As a result of the review the students draw up an immediate action plan which is implemented in the following week. This could involve catching up on missing work or working on additional tasks which cover the requirements of additional units. In addition they set longer range targets. After the two week hiatus the normal timetable restarts.

Review meetings in Art and Design take place in a room set aside during this fortnight for the purpose. It is comfortably furnished with easy chairs and contains the filing cabinets which hold the student records. In addition, it is close to the photocopier, enabling student records to be quickly updated, copied and refiled. Students have open access to their own files. The room also serves as the team meeting room and as a small seminar room used during normal teaching. It has no telephone!

This model is demanding in the sense that everyone on the course has to play their full part which requires both commitment and good communication. The course team meetings are essential in both respects. The general feeling is that everyone feels involved and understands what is going on. Much of the routine paperwork is completed by the students using the standard forms issued by BTEC for the purpose.

However, there is some concern that since the review process is concentrated into these two week blocks at half-termly intervals tutors are unavailable for one to one work with students in between review periods. Such individualised tutorials were needed with some students, especially at the beginning of the course, when tutors did make themselves available outside of normal teaching time though this again increased their work load substantially. One suggestion to tackle this issue is to increase tutorial time early on in the course at the expense of teaching time, with students being expected to do more on their own through the use of workshops. However, this is being resisted because of the need to support students in their learning of the vocational subjects early in the term. The debate still continues.

Case Study 3

In this FE college the senior management had given each team a certain number of hours in which to deliver their GNVQ and left each team to decide how they wanted to run their review meetings. I suspect, in fact, the senior management in this case were unaware that such reviews were an integral part of the course. The result over the four GNVQs I looked at was a whole range of different arrangements. Indeed in one case there was, initially, no provision for the student management of learning at all though this was changed after the first visit of the external verifier.

Induction varied from one day to half a term – with the result that one group of students seemed to have little idea of what they were doing – to another where several students had changed courses through the sheer frustration of not getting on with things. In addition the long induction period meant that the students had covered only two elements from two units and the course team was now being pushed for time.

The induction in two of the GNVQ courses was, however, excellent with students fully involved and learning about GNVQ by doing it. Here both course teams had produced excellent course handbooks in the form of ring binders to which the students were adding information as the course proceeded. These will be discussed further in the next chapter.

On-course review varied too. Two of the courses had gone for models very similar to that described in Case Study 2. One course seemed to have little review going on at all. Indeed the person designated as the personal tutor was using her time to teach extra science rather than conduct review meetings. The clear reason was that she did not see the point of the exercise and that her experience was entirely in teaching A level. Again the external verifier was able to convince her of the need for review meetings but the problems that this approach had set up with the students were never fully ironed out since their expectation of being taught was to act like sponges rather than to engage in dialogue about their own learning. Much of this can be traced back to an initial failure of this team, who were all teaching on vocational courses for the first time, to understand the rationale behind GNVQ.

The final course had produced a flexible approach to course review. By reducing overall class contact time the team had enabled themselves to double-staff one two-hour slot in the week where the personal tutor doubled up with the classroom teacher. This enabled the review process to go on formally at half-termly intervals but also provided the opportunity for students to talk with the personal tutor in between times. In addition students could also access the class teacher on an individual basis since the personal tutor could cover for her. All of this was only possible because the course tutor was sufficiently senior to negotiate this flexible timetable with her head of department and the agreement of the course team which developed flexible learning materials to enable the students to cope with the loss of classroom contact. The students clearly enjoyed the access to their tutor though:

> 'It's brilliant ... you can talk with her whenever you need to ...'
>
> 'When I need help I can get it without feeling embarrassed.'
>
> 'It really helped me being able to talk for an hour when things were going badly ...'

None of the models presented here is perfect. They can't be. Each has its drawbacks. The ones which seem to work the best though are those based on a course team approach, where there is agreement about the purpose of the review procedures, where there are jointly worked out and clearly understood procedures for reporting on student progress, and a proactive personal tutor who has the respect of the rest of the course team who involve students by encouraging them to take responsibility for managing their own learning.

In the following two chapters each stage of the review process is looked at in more detail again drawing on the work of real teachers, tutors and students to illustrate the main points. My own impression is that this process of managing student learning is central to running a successful GNVQ course. When done well it produces motivated students who understand what they are trying to achieve and want to learn.

Chapter 9

Student Enrolment and Pre-Course Counselling

The number of students studying GNVQ has grown at a staggering rate since their introduction in 1991. In 1993 about 8000 students completed GNVQ courses but by the summer of 1994 NCVQ estimated that this number would rise to 70 000. The rapid expansion of GNVQ has been the cause for some concern given the untried nature of the qualification and uncertainties about its currency with employers and higher education. None the less NCVQ are confident of achieving the Department for Education targets of 250 000 GNVQ students by 1997 and 50 per cent of the 16–19 age cohort taking GNVQs by the year 2000. Indeed the *Times Higher Education Supplement* (15.7.94) reported that 200 000 students would be taking GNVQ courses in 1994/95.

But who are these students? What are they like? What are their aspirations? Are their aspirations realistic? How can they be helped to choose the right course(s) and progression routes to meet those aspirations? These are the questions addressed in this chapter.

9.1 WHO ARE GNVQ STUDENTS?

The rapid rise in the number of GNVQ students is a reflection of the booming participation of young people in post-16 education which has occurred in the last few years. This rapid increase in post-16 full-time staying on has been fuelled, in the main, by students who would, traditionally, have left full-time education at 16 but are now staying on to continue their studies. Such students may have very different levels of prior educational achievement, needs and expectations to that more traditional group of young people who have stayed on – A level students. Furthermore, as the scope and range of GNVQs increases more and more students will come within this widening framework, producing a potentially very mixed cohort of students with an increasingly wide range of motivation, academic ability and vocational interest.

Students' aspirations

It is too easy to think that the motive for many students wanting to carry on with their education post-16 is simply that they cannot find a job. In fact the rapid rise in post-16 staying on rates started in 1988 at a time when unemployment was falling. Further, the available evidence suggests that the reasons for the increase are much more complex than unemployment and include:

- changes in parental and students' attitudes towards education and training
- a shift away from employing unskilled and unqualified young people at 16
- changes in the benefit rules so that young people can no longer claim benefit at 16
- the impact of GCSE and increased level of educational success pre-16.

This complexity is borne out by the reasons GNVQ students want to carry on with their studies. Discussions with GNVQ students in the first few weeks of a course also reveal something about their hopes and anxieties. The following points emerge from such discussions:

- GNVQ students want to carry on with their education and not simply attend a course because there is nothing else for them to do: 'I need to get better qualified. You need them [qualifications] to get a good job.' (Intermediate GNVQ Leisure and Tourism student)
- they often feel a sense of having failed at school which brings with it a lack of self-confidence and self-esteem: 'I didn't do well at school so I opted for this one [GNVQ course]. I'm not very good at it though.' – In fact his work was of a good standard. (Intermediate GNVQ Leisure and Tourism student)
- they often have a profound sense of inferiority compared with their more academically successful contemporaries: 'I wanted to do A levels but me GCSEs weren't good enough like so they told me to do this. All me mates are doing A level though.' (Advanced GNVQ Science student)
- they want to work and learn in a different way to the way they were taught at GCSE: 'I found out that GNVQ was more practical minded than GCSE and that the work experience which you did in the second year meant you could go and work in

industry. I think science is practical anyhow, when you actually do it you do experiments – you don't just read about it or write all the time like we did at GCSE.' (Advanced GNVQ Science student)

- they want their learning to be vocationally relevant: 'I've really liked the visits to the homes [nursing homes]. It made me realise what I was doing the course for.' (Intermediate GNVQ Health and Social Care student)
- they often choose GNVQ because of the emphasis on assignment and course work: 'I prefer doing course work and having tests after each section of work, than having to revise for a big test because with A levels it all depends on your last exam, and I get scared in exams!' (GNVQ Advanced Health and Social Care student)

You are therefore likely to get a fairly mixed bag of students coming to enrol on GNVQ courses. You are likely to meet:

- those who have been rejected for A level or other courses
- some who will have chosen your course because it is what they really want to do
- many will not know what they want to do other than continuing their education and they thought your course might be interesting.

The initial contact with students, before the courses even start, and the counselling which accompanies it is vital if students are going to be helped to make the right choices about their future. Furthermore, if you work in an FEFC sector institution such counselling is essential to prevent both student drop-out and failure to complete courses on time and so avoid the draconian financial penalties which accompany both of these outcomes.

9.2 SORTING STUDENTS

It is not easy to characterise such a very mixed group of students: indeed it would be fatuous to label them in simplistic ways. However, there are a few generalisations which can be made which may be useful to you in thinking through issues to do with precourse counselling.

Foundation GNVQ

There are so few foundation GNVQ students that it is difficult to say much about them. Several rationales as to the purpose of foundation GNVQ are plausible including:

- the provision of courses for those with special educational needs
- providing opportunities for students to sample across vocational areas. Foundation GNVQ allows greater flexibility in the way students can mix units than either intermediate or advanced GNVQ (see Figure 1.3a)
- provision for students for whom English is a second language.

Students who fall into such groups might therefore be directed towards Foundation GNVQ but there may be a feeling amongst students and parents that this is a low-level qualification and one with little currency. Whilst it is difficult to see the currency of Foundation GNVQ, other than as a stepping-stone to other courses, it should not be dismissed as an easy option. Indeed no GNVQ is an easy option: in many ways they are far more demanding qualifications than GCSE or A level. None the less, ethical questions about enrolling students on Foundation GNVQ do remain, including:

- Why am I enrolling this student on this course? How, exactly, will they benefit from a further year in full-time education?
- What, realistically, are the progression opportunities for this student?
- Might this student be better served by entering, or attempting to enter, the labour market, and improving their qualifications through, for example, the NVQ route?

These questions are, perhaps, relevant to any student seeking to enrol on any course. Counselling which is ethical requires such hard questions to be addressed. Education should not, I believe, be seen as a panacea for all the problems of society and some students may best be served by leaving full-time, formal education at 16 to follow alternative pathways. The dilemma for lecturers and teachers enrolling students is how to maintain such an ethical stance in the face of the increasing commercialisation and commodification of education. In a world of targets, money following students and competition between post-16 education providers, how easy is it to provide unbiased, impartial advice which may result in a potential student not enrolling on your course?

Intermediate GNVQ

In most institutions Intermediate GNVQ students tend to be those who have performed less well at GCSE, for whatever reason. They are often looking either for a bridging course to other educational opportunities, e.g. advanced GNVQ, or a qualification which will enable them to find a job. There are also a significant number who do not really know what they want to do. This group of undecided, and vocationally uncommitted, students is potentially problematic in the context of more vocationally focused courses like Intermediate GNVQ.

Potential Intermediate GNVQ students are, therefore, likely to be a very mixed bag. Some will be similar to BTEC First students and will be vocationally focused: they have chosen your course because they want a career in that vocational area. But a surprising number have no real idea what they want to do. Some may have achieved much poorer GCSE results than they expected and so were unable to enrol on the advanced course they wanted. For them the Intermediate GNVQ may be a stepping stone to Advanced GNVQ or a way to continue their studies for a year. For these students, who do not have a clear idea of what they want to do, being forced to choose an occupational area to study at 16 may be a weakness of Intermediate GNVQ. They may simply end up doing something they do not really know enough about and they may therefore make an inappropriate choice.

Such students were, in the past, well served by qualifications like the Diploma of Vocational Education (DoVE) which allowed students to sample across a range of occupational areas. The Foundation GNVQ also offers such an opportunity for sampling but this may be an inappropriate starting-point for these undecided students.

The practical implications of this are that these undecided students need especially careful counselling before enrolling on a GNVQ course to ensure they are making an informed decision. Furthermore, they need to be carefully monitored in the first few weeks of a course to ensure that the course is still meeting their needs. An early exposure to the sorts of occupations they might enter with the qualification is also a good idea:

> I didn't really know what I wanted to do when I came to college and I didn't get much help from my school. But the college advisers were great. They took time to explain things and how I could change course if I wanted. I guess I chose

> Health and Social Care because it sounded interesting. In the first week we had to go on a visit to an old people's home. It was brilliant ... it made me realise that I really wanted to work with people and that the course I was on was the right one. (Intermediate GNVQ Health and Social Care student)

Even students who think they know what to do may change their mind:

> When I came I thought business sounded right for me. But I found the work really boring and hard. When I went to work in an office for two days as part of my first assignment I realised that this was not for me. I talked with my tutors and the advisers and I changed to Health and Social Care. I am much happier now that I am doing the right thing. (Intermediate Health and Social Care student)

KEY IDEA: Intermediate GNVQ is a much more stark choice for undecided students than previous qualifications. Counselling prior to enrolment and in the early stages of a course to ensure that these students have made the correct decision is essential.

Advanced GNVQ

It would be easy to characterise Advanced GNVQ students as those who have not got sufficient GCSE passes at grade C or above to do A level. To be sure many GNVQ students would fit into this category but this is not the whole story. There are, for example, some students who want to do GNVQ rather than A level courses even though they have the GCSE grades to do the latter. At Coventry Technical College, for example, one lecturer, Colin Butler, reports that of the students taking the advanced GNVQs in Health and Social Care and Science 'many have better GCSE grades than many of our current A level students' (*Times Educational Supplement*, 29.9.93). Evidence from other institutions also suggests that GNVQ courses are 'very popular with those brighter students who find A levels boring and undemanding' (*Times Educational Supplement*, 26.11.93).

At other colleges advanced GNVQ has been found to provide increased flexibility for those students who know they want to take one A level but not others. For example, in one college some students taking Geography A level were also taking Advanced Science GNVQ to provide them with both a complete timetable and, more importantly, a broad course which complemented their A level studies.

By and large Advanced GNVQ students do seem to have a well-developed vocational focus and fitting them to courses does not appear to be especially problematic. The one exception are those students who have set their heart on doing A level but who do not have the necessary GCSEs. Recent evidence from the Audit Commission, OFSTED and official government statistics strongly suggests that students with low points scores, below about 30, in GCSE do not do well at A level. It is this group where there is a disproportionately high drop-out and failure rate. Of course you will always get exceptions to the rule but the financial penalties incurred for non completion of courses by institutions who come under the Further Education and Funding Council are now severe and have to be taken into account when enrolling a student. There is no one way of dealing with the would-be A level student with poor GCSE grades other than talking and applying the policy laid down by senior managers. For some of these students the one A level plus Advanced GNVQ might be the best option.

The other interesting group are those students who have got the correct GCSEs for doing a three A levels course but who are not sure that is what they want to do. Here the problem might be that whilst these students find the GNVQ course inherently more appealing they do have to realise that entrance to Higher Education may be more reliable if they take A levels rather than GNVQ at least until HE becomes more familiar with GNVQ students. Here, then, you need to take account of both the qualifications the student has and their final aspirations. At the moment the A level route, though a higher risk than the GNVQ route, still has higher status and provides the wider range of options for entry into HE. Hopefully this will change over time.

9.3 PRE-ENROLMENT COUNSELLING

The exact details of enrolment procedures are likely to be determined by your institution but it is quite likely that you will be involved in selecting students for your course. If you are working in a school you will have considerable background information to call on, especially your own knowledge of potential students. For example, one community school I have talked to identifies prospective GNVQ students as being those who do well on course work assessment but less well in terminal or modular exams.

Even so students who have been counselled at the end of year 11 may change their minds as a result of their GCSE results or their experiences over the summer holidays. So pre-course counselling in school is still strongly recommended to ensure that students have really made the right choice. The corrosive influence of a student doing the wrong GNVQ is very apparent and wearing for all concerned.

If you are working in a post-16 establishment you may have a more difficult time than your colleagues in school. You may not know the students unless you have been involved with the preliminary interviews. The first time you see them may be when they come to enrol and that process is such a rush that it is often difficult to find time to talk with them. It is all too easy to enrol students who know what they want to do and have the appropriate qualifications on the course of their choice without taking time to check if they are making a wise decision. Such students can often cause problems later. The undecided ones are easier to deal with in the sense that they identify themselves. How they are dealt with will of course depend upon the institutional arrangements where you work. One college's response is described below. The key elements, though, are time and talk.

9.4 PRE-ENROLMENT COUNSELLING: A CASE STUDY

All the prospective students at this college have a minimum entitlement of a one to one interview with a lecturer who teaches on the type of course they want to take before they enrol. For GNVQ students this means a member of the course team. All students coming for enrolment are asked to bring with them information about their previous achievements in the form of certificates, Records of Achievement, action plans and so on. Enrolment cannot proceed without this documentation. Students can be accompanied by their parents but this can present problems since the interviewing lecturer can often end up talking with the parent rather than the prospective student. Lecturers have a senior and experienced member of staff from their section available to advise and assist them during the interviewing process. This is essential, especially for inexperienced or new lecturers.

Dealing with the undecided students

A special 'desk' is set up for students who do not know what they want to do, which acts as a clearing centre. The desk is personed by a range of staff including college advisers, careers staff and lecturers from specialist areas. Prospective students arrive at the desk by one of two routes: directly because they do not know what they want to do or by referral from the initial face to face interview with another member of staff. This latter category of students are those who thought they knew what they wanted to do but have found that they either do not have the appropriate qualifications for the course they have chosen or have realised, after talking with the interviewing member of staff, that they do not actually want to do the described course. Such students can be especially difficult to deal with since they are often resentful of not having been offered the course of their choice.

Students presenting themselves at the desk are taken to quiet rooms for an individual consultation with one or more members of staff. Such consultations can be quite extensive and may last up to 30 minutes. The objective is to get the prospective student to talk about themselves, their aspirations and interests. The additional counselling skills of the college advisers are important here. On the basis of this conversation the student is then given information about the range of courses for which they might apply and for which they are qualified. Again this can be a difficult procedure since students may have aspirations to courses for which they do not have the necessary qualifications. This was most often manifested in students who wanted to do A level but did not have the GCSE grades required by the subject. For those students who really did not have a clear idea about what they wanted to do the degree of vagueness ranged from 'something to do with cars', 'I want to work with people', through to 'I haven't got a clue'.

The outcome of the conversation was a preferred first choice of course with a back-up option. Sometimes prospective students wanted to go away and have a think. Such students were provided with a time for a further interview. Those who had made up their mind were then directed to the subject area desks to enrol on the course. They were provided with a brief summary of the conversation that had taken place and the outcome of that conversation. This was signed by all concerned. Upon enrolment this piece of paper was placed in the student's folder so it was available for reference by the course and personal tutor.

The system was elaborate and time consuming but the senior

managers claimed that it had significantly reduced college drop-out and failure by ensuring that students were better matched to courses. Given changes to the way post-16 institutions are funded by the Further Education Funding Counsel (FEFC) the senior college managers felt this was money well spent.

Student feelings

However, the real importance of this pre-course counselling for me was the impact it had on the GNVQ students. Many of the students had felt they had done less well than they hoped at GCSE and they were often relieved to find the doors of further education had not closed for them. Given that many of the students were shy and lacked confidence the efforts made by the college and the lecturers to make them feel comfortable were appreciated. The opportunity to talk and have someone take seriously what they were saying was also acknowledged. Even at this early stage of their college careers GNVQ students were, therefore, meeting the essential elements of good management of learning on GNVQ courses:

- a student-centred approach
- using information about previous achievement to map out future learning opportunities
- the opportunity for students and lecturers to talk at length, on a one to one basis and in confidence
- the development of an agreed plan of action (action plan)
- recording of conversations for future reference by both parties and to ensure targets set are being met.

Developing a partnership

This requires the teachers and lecturers involved to deploy additional skills. In particular the capacity to listen and help the prospective student to talk about themselves. Many teachers I have spoken to, especially those who have worked on vocational courses before, have remarked how difficult they have found this.

> Traditionally students listen to teachers and we decide what goes on. But now I have to listen much more to my students. I guess we are forming more of a partnership. (New GNVQ science teacher)

At the heart of this partnership, which begins with pre-course counselling, seems to be the idea of treating GNVQ students as young, responsible adults who are making decisions for themselves. Of course the extent to which the partnership develops depends on both the teacher and the student. Some students are very immature and find it difficult to take responsibility. Some teachers find it hard to let go and encourage students to take responsibility. If managing a student's learning is going to be successful both sides of the partnership have got to take the process seriously, work at it and learn from each other. The initial stages of a course are essential for setting the tone of the environment in which the partnership develops. It is that we turn to first in the final chapter.

Chapter 10

Induction and Action Planning

In this the final chapter two processes which lie at the heart of the management of student learning, induction and action planning are examined in some detail. The first involves getting the course and the students off to a good start. The second maintains the impetus, helping students to realise the central importance in GNVQ of taking responsibility for their own learning and organising their portfolios. Successful action planning during review sessions is also the mechanism which helps to maintain the flow of information so central to the model of learning management developed in this third section of the book.

10.1 INDUCTION: WHAT YOU HAVE TO DO

All the awarding bodies and NCVQ attach importance to the notion of student induction:

> It is very important that institutions offering GNVQ should provide induction programmes in which potential students can become fully familiar with the nature of GNVQs and the range of units on offer. (Royal Society of Arts (1993b) p20)

> It is advisable that institutions offering GNVQs should provide induction programmes. (NCVQ (1993a) p11)

This view is supported by teachers from pilot centres:

> You must have an induction programme, properly planned to familiarise students with the new scheme and new processes. (PSSI (1994) p5)

> I realised after half a term following a conversation with our external verifier that I had not paid enough attention to induction. I shall start next half term with another induction programme which will help the students understand what it is they are supposed to be doing. (Intermediate Leisure and Tourism teacher)

Clearly, then, an induction programme is necessary but

- what form should such a programme take?
- what is its purpose?
- how long should it last?
- what sorts of things need explaining and how?
- how should it be managed?

As with most other aspects of GNVQ designing, the induction programme should be a course team activity. The next few pages will help you think about the purpose of induction and how it can be managed but you should then put this thinking to collaborative use.

Rationale

The BTEC documentation provides the most detailed rationale for the function of induction in GNVQ courses:

> It serves to:
>
> - encourage the learner to reflect upon their achievement to date
> - identify learner needs
> - allow the negotiation of individual learning programmes
> - allow the learner to become familiar with their learning programme and environment. (BTEC (1993a) p31)

However, whilst such aims, emphasising as they do a process of both looking back and looking forward, seem laudable on paper, the issue is how practical are they in your institution and with your group of students. How do you as a teacher help young learners to 'reflect upon achievements to date' or 'negotiate an individual learning programme'? Indeed what exactly is an individual learning programme and how do you construct one? What can happen is that teachers feel unable to operationalise these aims and so ignore them and get on with what they do best: teaching their subject. However, that can lead to disaster.

> I realise now that the year started off on entirely the wrong foot. I did not give the students time to familiarise themselves with the demands of the new course, largely I think because I did not know what they were myself. I just sat them down and got on with teaching them the content. As a result they have become very passive learners and now are finding it difficult to produce the evidence of planning and evaluating their

work needed to achieve the higher grades. I feel this is my fault. (Intermediate GNVQ Health and Social Care teacher)

Students need to realise at the beginning of the course that GNVQ is different: a course which is not only vocationally relevant but one where they will be expected to take much more responsibility for their own learning.

KEY IDEA: Induction should make students aware that they will be working in new ways.

Thinking about learning

A prime concern during induction is the need to make students more aware of and take responsibility for their learning. This is not easy. Many A level students, for example, equate their learning with the passive accumulation of a file of notes largely taken from the board or by dictation: 'A good lesson ... that's when I write down a lot, a lot of notes ... I know what I've got then.' (A level biology student)

Such an approach will not work with GNVQ but this is what students might be expecting from the course. For example, GNVQ advanced science students interviewed as part of the NCVQ's evaluation of the science pilot found it very difficult to understand that they were learning anything because they were not making vast amounts of notes and were not engaged in teacher-directed activities.

KEY IDEA: During induction students must be helped to see how they are learning from new ways of working.

So how do you get students to be more aware of their own learning? This is not easy. Essentially you have got to get them to talk about learning. However, if you simply ask them how do you think you learn they are unlikely to give you a satisfactory answer for a number of reasons including:

- the question is too abstract
- they will probably never have thought about learning in a formal way before
- they may equate learning solely with learning in a formal academic way in school.

You are likely to make more progress if you ask them concrete questions about specific incidents:

- how did you learn to get to school?
- how did you learn to write?
- how did you learn to swim?
- how did you learn to ride a bike?
- how did you learn to do your part-time job?

More complex approaches use strategies like concept maps, group discussion and brainstorming.

Using such approaches will make students aware of how much they have already learnt, how they learn all the time both in and outside of school or college, the resources they have used to learn things and the way they have gone about it. However, this approach does require some one to one contact, and considerable patience and encouragement from the teacher that what the students are saying is neither trivial not unimportant. None the less you are meeting the first aim set out by BTEC above 'Encouraging learners to reflect upon achievement to date'.

Identifying learning needs

If you have access to the student's National Record of Achievement (NRA) this can also be very useful since it gives you concrete examples of achievement which you can talk about. The one to one nature of the relationship not only gives you a chance to get to know the pupil but gives them a chance to get to know you which is going to be essential in the future.

Looking through the NRA with individual students will also help you to 'identify learner needs' albeit in a crude way. For example does the evidence in the NRA and/or from your discussion with the student suggest this student might have poor literacy or numeracy skills. Early identification of potential problems in these two key core skill areas, through initial assessment, is fundamental since:

- these are major sources of low self-esteem and low self-confidence
- it alerts you to the need to provide specific help for this student in these areas, perhaps through learning support workshops
- it may enable you to negotiate with the student to enable them to produce evidence of vocational achievement in different ways other than purely in writing.

This last point is clearly an example of 'negotiation of individual learning programmes'. For example one GNVQ intermediate teacher encouraged some of her Intermediate Business Students initially to produce evidence of achievement in the form of video tapes and tape recordings rather than the written reports being produced by other students because they were poor writers. The need to improve handwriting and spelling was, however, recognised and the students attended the college literacy workshop where they concentrated on developing their spelling and handwriting skills outside of normal class time. Since the students had been involved from the outset in negotiating this with their tutor they appreciated the importance of improving their handwriting in order to gain jobs in an office environment, so they were motivated to improve. By Christmas they were producing evidence in the same way as the other students, including the production of written evidence.

Introducing the course

This still leaves the last of the aims made explicit by BTEC: 'allow the learner to become familiar with their learning programme and environment'. Clearly one aspect of this is the highly individualised and interactive relationship they are going to enjoy with you through the course of the programme. The importance of getting this message over early on in the course cannot be emphasised enough. They must know that they can come to you, ask questions about their work, ask for tutorial support.

KEY IDEA: Induction needs to develop a close working relationship between teachers and students.

However, students will also need to become familiar with the structure of GNVQ and the way it is assessed. In short they have to be taught to 'speak' GNVQ. This will include:

Familiarisation with:

- The learning environment, both the physical resources they are going to be using, for example classrooms, libraries and workshops, plus the way of working. If the students are new to the institution they will also need to know where to find the toilets, student common room, dining room and so on. A good induction assignment is to get them making a map of the buildings they will be working in.
- The GNVQ programme team, including the core skills teachers. Photographs of everyone, including the students are useful

here. A good ice-breaker is the guess who they are game using photographs of them and yourself as babies
- The GNVQ programme, including specifications of mandatory units, core skill units, optional and additional units which may be offered
- Assessment strategies
- Grading criteria
- Recording and tracking documentation
- Appeals procedure

Introduction to:

- Developing portfolios of evidence
- Developing action plans
- The tutorial support systems
- Their role in the programme
- The role of work experience
- Opportunities for progression

Again this is a daunting list and as one awarding body helpfully points out:

> The way in which students are introduced to these is, of course, a matter of judgement for the staff, but they should all be available at an early stage. (Royal Society of Arts (1993b) p20)

10.2 MODELS OF INDUCTION

The list above tells you what you have to do during induction but not how to do it. If you think about it from the students' point of view you will begin to appreciate the problems. They have got to learn the language of GNVQ (remember what a struggle that was for you!), and they have got to learn to work in new ways. Your job as a teacher is to help them do this but without terrifying them or boring them off your course. Three possible models are suggested below. All are stereotypes but they are based on observations and/or discussions with teachers from a range of institutions.

Model 1: The block of time approach

The notion of induction suggests it is an activity that comes at the beginning of the course, before you start doing anything else. One obvious way to approach induction would, therefore, be to put it as a block of time at the beginning of the course. Given that you have a lot to get through it would need to be a substantial block of time, perhaps two weeks. During that time you would tell the students about all the things on the list above, go through all the mandatory and core skill units with them, explaining about performance criteria, range and so on as you went. At the end of two weeks you could then get on with the teaching.

Whilst this model is highly structured and ensures *you* have covered all the things listed earlier the effects on the students may be the exact opposite of what you expect:

- students leave, not because they do not like the course, but because they find induction irrelevant and boring, they want to get on with the work
- the way of working, i.e. highly teacher-centred, reinforces students' expectations about learning, i.e. learning equals 'sit, passively listen and write for most of the time'
- students fail to understand GNVQ-speak because they have no direct experience of using the performance or grading criteria for example
- the one to one contact between teachers and students is not developed
- early diagnosis of learning needs is not achieved.

Of course students need to be told things but experience suggests that this approach on its own does not provide an appropriate induction experience for GNVQ students.

Model 2: The student handbook approach

All the information that the students need to have about GNVQ and the institution, staff, ways of working and so on are set out in the student handbook. In one extreme case all the assignments were also included, resulting in a document of nearly one hundred double sided A4 pages. The students are then given a brief introduction to the course which might last only one morning and then teaching starts. The assumption is that the students will read the handbook, understand what they have read and so come to grips with GNVQ and its way of working. I suspect the fate of many of these expensively produced documents is to end up in the bottom of students' bags where they remain. It certainly does not seem to have the desired effect: students do not know how GNVQ works, they do not understand about their role, they have certainly not had their learning needs diagnosed or individual learning programmes negotiated. Nor have they had that essential early one to one contact with their tutor. This is not to say that a student handbook is not essential, it is, but it is not sufficient on its own.

Model 3: The assignment approach

This model attempts to deal with induction by using the methods of working which students will normally be using on the course. Students work through a set of induction assignments which are designed not so much to generate evidence for assessment, though they will, but to teach students how to work in GNVQ by doing it. Good induction assignments:

- are vocationally focused: students feel they are getting on with work which interests them
- are short: students can get rapid feedback on their work
- involve students in planning and evaluating right from the start of the course: students realise they will be working in new ways
- provide feedback using performance criteria and grading criteria: students start to learn and use the language of GNVQ
- provide feedback on a one to one or small group basis: students develop close relationships with tutors
- are often small group activities; students learn to co-operate
- encourage students to present evidence using a range of methods
- emphasise core skills: student problems in key areas are diagnosed early and individual learning programmes negotiated
- encourage reflection on what has been learnt and how: students think about their own learning
- minimise, even trivialise the knowledge component: students enjoy early success.

The advantages of this method are, I hope, obvious, but if adhered to strictly this can be a very dry diet, a treadmill of one assignment after another. In addition, students will be unused to working in this way and will need considerable encouragement, so it will be a drain on your energies, and it will certainly foster feelings of insecurity, 'Am I doing the right thing?', in both the students and yourself. Clearly if you are going to adopt this strategy then you do need to break it up perhaps by, for example, your covering some vocational content in a formal way, and the strategy needs to be implemented in a planned and structured way. Furthermore, the strategy only has the desired effect if you spend a lot of time talking to students on a one to one basis, encouraging them to use the GNVQ criteria, getting them to think about how they are learning and so on.

Finally it can also be very time consuming if you try to cover all of the things on the list given at the end of section 10.1 using assignments and you will begin to worry about having enough time to cover the knowledge and understanding demanded in the rest of the course. One way around this is to actually reconceptualise the notion of induction so that you see it not as one block of time but a continuous process throughout the course. You introduce new elements of understanding about GNVQ as and when your students need them using a little assignment. This 'Just in time' approach ensures that the students use their new learning about GNVQ immediately, so reinforcing it.

To conclude, induction is essential for students to help them understand what GNVQ is about and especially to impress on them that they are going to be much more involved and play a more active part in planning and evaluating their work than they have hitherto done. Consequently induction needs very careful planning, with a clear set of aims and a lot of structure: it should not be a student free-for-all with each student doing what they want. What you do need though is an induction programme which will motivate and excite your students, make them realise they are going to be doing something different and help them to understand the new ways in which they are going to be learning, especially the active part they will be expected to take. I would argue that the best way to do this is to get them actively involved in the induction process so they learn about GNVQ by doing it.

10.3 ACTION PLANNING: ADVICE FROM AWARDING BODIES

This process lies at the heart of running on-course review sessions and the term appears again and again within the documentation supplied by the awarding bodies. Clearly it is seen by all three to be central to the successful management of GNVQ students' learning. What is less clear is what the process actually involves. For example:

> GNVQ candidates will be involved in individual programmes of activity based learning. A young candidate will usually have a National Record of Achievement with an individual action

> plan which indicates the candidate's intentions for further education and training. Many candidates will make plans well into the future.
>
> Individual action planning is important to all GNVQ programmes as it is a record of candidates' intentions. All centres must have arrangements for building on candidates' action plans.
>
> A candidate's action plan should be reviewed during induction and at appropriate intervals through the GNVQ programme. It should consider the short-, medium- and long-term, but tutors must be aware that a period which one candidate believes to be long-term might be medium-term for others.
>
> The action plan should take into account where candidates perceive themselves in relation to a particular goal or set of goals and give appropriate time scales for achieving those goals. It should tell how the candidate can move forward and the amount of and type of support which the candidate might need to help his or her chances of success. (City and Guilds (1993) p23)

The BTEC guidelines are a little more specific and see action planning as an integral part of the process of learning:

> The role of action planning is to empower the learner to determine, manage and review his/her learning process. Action plans need to be regularly reviewed and used as a basis for involving the learner in planning and discussing openly his/her current skills, knowledge and understanding. This process enables both learner and tutor to set realistic targets for each stage in the learning process at entry, on programme, and at exit. (BTEC (1993a) p29)

BTEC also identify the rationale for action planning at the three different stages of a GNVQ course (Table 10.1) and identify two sorts of action plan, forward plans and assessment activity plans, rather than just one which a student will need to draw up during a GNVQ course. The first of these was discussed in Chapter 3 so it is the latter, longer range planning which is of concern here. Finally RSA stress the importance of Action Plans in assessment and learning:

Table 10.1 *The purposes of action planning (Implementing BTEC GNVQs) p.29)*

At Entry	On Programme	At Exit
Action planning: • Identifies appropriate induction programme • Identifies learning and assessment plans • Sets targets for the early stages in the learning programme	*Action planning:* • Planning for learning, using a forward plan • Planning for assessment, using an assessment activity action plan (see Chapter 3)	*Action planning:* • Reflects on achievements • Identifies pathways for progression to further education, higher education, training and employment

> Assessment Action Plans should be used to develop the student's ability to plan their own learning and assessment. Plans should set out the targets for learning and assessment in the form of units to be claimed and the activities that will be undertaken to produce evidence of achievement for the units. (Royal Society of Arts (1993b) p21)

Teachers, language and action planning

These are good ideas but the language in which they are couched is alien to many teachers who do not conceive of the job they do in terms of negotiating individualised learning programmes through action planning. The strangeness of the language almost inevitably leads to confusion which is further compounded by the fact that the awarding bodies do not say how action planning should be organised, what form it should take, what should be covered in an action planning session. The effect of such confusion can lead to teachers ignoring action planning altogether:

> We have used the time given to us [for review sessions] to get on and teach the knowledge which the students need to cover for the Unit tests. (GNVQ Advanced Science co-ordinator)

Further discussion revealed that this particular lecturer admitted that he had not really understood what action planning was about and did not feel confident that he had the skills necessary to carry out the sort of one to one work with students that action planning requires. This is not a trivial problem but is typical of a situation where teachers are exhorted to do something without having the rationale explained to them.

Why action plan?

Action planning is, however, important since it enables students to become more involved in planning their work; evaluating their work; and planning for the future on the basis of this evaluation, and these are part of the grading criteria for GNVQ. Put bluntly the chances of your students achieving the higher grades of GNVQ without effective action planning are minimal.

10.4 ACTION PLANNING: CASE STUDIES

In institutions where action planning is effective it gives the course a structure which supports the students in the active learning required for success in GNVQs. There is, as the following case studies make clear, not just one way of organising action planning. Rather it is a question of your devising the method which suits your institution and students best. However, the important point about all the institutions discussed in the case studies is that they had all placed an enormous importance to the process of action planning and they were certainly not paying lip service to it.

Case Study 1: A centralised model in an FE college

This college was used to running BTEC National Diploma programmes and had altered the programme they had used with these courses to provide an action planning programme for all their GNVQ courses which was the same, i.e. a centrally imposed model. Every five weeks throughout the course the timetable was suspended for one week, designated a review week. All action planning was supposed to take place in this week.

During this time students would collect together all the work they had done since the previous review week and they would discuss what they had done and achieved with a designated tutor. This meant that the students on a course would be spread amongst the staff making up the course team so that any one member of staff would only have a few students to deal with during the week. But each member of staff would have to be prepared to review work done across the whole of an occupational area even when that work came from an area they were not familiar with.

Action planning was divided in two sessions each lasting one hour. Students were expected to work independently of staff when not involved in review discussions.

The first session involved students presenting the work they had done in the previous four weeks. This provided the tutor with the opportunity to ensure the students were up to date with their work and to ensure that all the necessary paper work, for example assignment cover sheets, had been completed by each student and the respective tutor(s). Any work which had not been completed was identified and the student was expected to complete it by the time of the second session later in the week. The amount of time taken up by this process is considerable. Any remaining time in the first session was then used for discussing the student's achievements in the past four weeks.

The second session was much more concerned with target-setting. After ensuring that work which had not been completed was up to date the tutor and student would continue their discussion of student progress using the criteria set out by GNVQ and the action plans devised in the previous review week. Such discussions were very wide ranging and often ended up as counselling sessions rather than strictly action planning sessions relating solely to the student's work. For example, students might wish to discuss personal problems or their career aspirations during these sessions. The result was that these discussions could become very unfocused but this was resolved by the use of documentation which ensured that the outcome of the discussion was a written record which summarised:

- what the student had achieved since the last review session in terms of elements, performance criteria and range from the GNVQ units. This information was then transferred to the Vocational Tracking sheets
- core skills tracking sheets were completed
- if a unit had been completed successfully, including passing the external or internal test, this was signed off on the qualification summary which was filed at the front of the student's portfolio
- the Index to the Portfolio of Evidence was then updated.

Examples of completed documentation for one intermediate GNVQ student after the second review are shown in Figure 10.1. This was the documentation completed during the first action planning session and formed the basis for the more substantive discussion of progress in the next session. The outcomes of this were also recorded in the form of an action plan for both the student and the tutor. The matching example for the same student discussed above is shown in Figure 10.2. Notice how both past work and future work are being discussed, with activities to be undertaken in the next five weeks identified. The need to meet deadlines is starting to be appreciated and opportunities identified in future assignments for development of core skills (Application of Number and IT). This student has a specific problem with numeracy and so another visit to the maths workshop is arranged. Finally a date for the next review meeting is agreed.

The process being used here seems to fit the aim of action planning as specified by the three awarding bodies well in that:

- existing skills and those developed since the last review are determined
- goals to be achieved in the next five weeks are identified
- how those goals are to be achieved, in particular the learning needs of the student are identified, especially the need for extra help with numeracy

HIGHCLERE COLLEGE

INTERMEDIATE GNVQ VOCATIONAL TRACKING SHEET

NAME: John Smith **PERSONAL TUTOR:** Mrs. Grey

COURSE: Health & Social Care **UNIT:** Health Emergencies

Assignment	Ref. No.	Element 1			Element 2					Element 3			
		1.1	1.2	1.3	2.1	2.2	2.3	2.4	2.5	3.1	3.2	3.3	3.4
First Aid	HSC 2 3/1	✓	✓	✓	✓	✓	✓	✓	✓	✓	✓	✓	✓
Crash	HSC 2 3/3	✓	✓	✓	✓	✓	✓		✓	✓	✓	✓	
Hospital visit	HSC 2 3/4									✓	✓	✓	✓
CPR course	HSC 2 3/5	✓					✓						

	Element 1	Element 2	Element 3
	Range Covered: YES	Range Covered: YES	Range Covered: YES
External Test Passed:	Element achieved Assessor: A. Sharp Date: 26/11/93	Element achieved Assessor: A. Sharp Date: 26/11/93	Element achieved Assessor: A. Sharp Date: 3/12/93

10.1(a) *A completed tracking sheet to show elements achieved during one cycle of learning. Notice how there are several opportunities for a student to succeed by ensuring coverage of the same element in different activities.*

HIGHCLERE COLLEGE

INTERMEDIATE GNVQ CORE SKILLS TRACKING SHEET

NAME: John Smith **COURSE:** Health & Social Care

PERSONAL TUTOR: Mrs J. Grey

GNVQ CORE SKILLS UNIT: COMMUNICATION

Element 1: Take part in discussions with a range of people on routine matters

PC1	PC2	PC3	PC4
Evidence: **First aid course** **CPR course**	Evidence: **First aid course** **CPR course**	Evidence: **First aid course** **CPR course**	Evidence: **First aid course** **CPR course**

Element 2: Prepare written material on routine matters

PC1	PC2	PC3	PC4
Evidence:	Evidence:	Evidence:	Evidence:

Element 3: Use images to illustrate points made in writing and in discussions with a range of people on routine matters

PC1	PC2	PC3
Evidence:	Evidence:	Evidence:

Element 4: Read and respond to written materials and images on routine matters

PC1	PC2
Evidence:	Evidence:

10.1(b) *A core skills tracking sheet. This student has achieved the first element of the communications unit at level 2.*

HIGHCLERE COLLEGE

INDEX TO GNVQ PORTFOLIO OF EVIDENCE

NAME: John Smith **GNVQ COURSE:** Health & Social Care
PERSONAL TUTOR: Mrs J.Grey

Ref. No.	Assignment	What you achieved	Grades	Date
HSC2 3/1	First Aid	Elements 1, 2, 3 Unit 3 - All range except health and safety bit Element 3	Pass	26/11/ 93
HSC 2 3/3	Crash	Element 1, All PCs Element 2, PC 2.1, 2.2, 2.3, 2.5 Element 3, PC 3.1, 3.2, 3.3 Range: some emergencies; safety needs of those attending	Pass	26/11/ 93
HSC 2 3/4	Hospital visit	Element 3 Range: All	Merit for planning	3/12/ 93
HSC 2 3/5	CPR course	Element 1 PC1 Element 2 PC3 Range to do with heart attack	Pass	8/12/ 93

10.1(c) *Portfolio index sheet to show where evidence is located within the portfolio.*

Figure 10.1 *A completed set of recording documents from the first review session in one college. These are all tracking documents which help students, assessors and verifiers to navigate through a portfolio. Again these were developed from documents supplied by the awarding body.*

GNVQ REVIEW SHEET

Name John Smith

Review period: Oct - Dec 1993

Since the last review I have achieved:

Unit 3 - all elements passed. Evidence in my portfolio.

Element 1 of communication unit passed.

I have been to the maths work shop 5 times. I can now use the Apple computer, word processing and drawing.

Gained my CPR certificate. Gained my First Aid Certificate

By the next review I will have

Completed assignment for Units 1 and 2

Have learnt to use a spread sheet by going to the IT workshop

Set up a data base from survey data on assignment in Unit 2. This will help me with application of number. Survey needs to be done over Christmas.

Learning support needed:

I think I still need more help with maths. I need this to help with the survey.

John is still having trouble with basic numerical problems.

Access to workshops:

Access for John no problem. Just needs to turn up with work from survey.

Chris to help with IT.

Next review will be on: 14/2
At: 11.30

Signatures:
Student:

Tutor:

Figure 10.2 *A completed review sheet. This was used as the basis for a discussion in, and completed during, a review session. The comments were originally handwritten but have been typed here to aid clarity. The teacher's comments are shown in italic. This was an early review session and the student was still having difficulty in commenting on their own performance and identifying their own learning needs. This written record provides a limited view of the more important discussion process between the student and the personal tutor in the review session.*

- arrangements to provide learning support are made, e.g. in this case, extra visits to the maths workshop
- assessment opportunities and activities are identified.

In addition the process has also given the tutor a set of aims. In this college these are communicated to the rest of the course team and each student's progress and future plans reviewed at a course team meeting. The process works well for this college but to make it work requires:

- a team approach to delivering GNVQ
- the fact that all members of the course team are willing to act as tutors
- the provision of time by senior management for tutorial purposes.

However, the system does have its drawbacks. This method of working can become very bureaucratic with paperwork rather than talking being seen as the main purpose of the action planning sessions. In addition the concentration of action planning activities in these weekly slots means that some students do not receive sufficient tutorial support in the intervening weeks when the tutors' attention is focused more on subject teaching and supporting subject work. This causes frustration amongst both staff and students:

> Sometimes when I need to speak to someone about my work or a problem I have to wait until the review week but I need help now. (GNVQ Business student)

> We put so much effort into tutorial work in review weeks that I feel I cannot spend time with students on a one to one basis in between. As a result problems can pile up. I think we probably need to give the students more opportunities to talk to us between review weeks. (GNVQ Business lecturer)

This sort of approach seems therefore to give a sort of stop-start feel to the action planning process rather than a feeling of continuous review and dialogue between students and staff. Interestingly it was a scheme imposed from above by senior managers looking to ensure that they met the requirements of the awarding body, but the system, whilst having many strengths, did not seem to meet all the needs of the students who at this early stage in the course felt they needed more tutorial support, nor the feelings of the staff who were implementing it.

Case Study 2: A cyclical approach

This centre had appointed one member of the course team to be the tutor for all the students on a particular GNVQ course and had allocated two hours per week tutorial support. Each course team had then been left to decide how they wanted to use this time. The team considered here had gone for a programme of tutorials where each student was seen once every six weeks by the individual tutor for reviews and action planning. Since there were eleven students on the course this meant that each student only received one hour every six weeks. However, other course team members were playing an active part in the process by ensuring the students were staying up to date with assignments and by providing detailed written comments about the students work in the form of an assignment cover sheet.

It was these cover sheets which formed the basis of the review procedure. Less time was spent on maintaining the portfolio: the students were given more responsibility for this. Rather the time was spent on discussing progress, problems the student was having and ways of overcoming these. Each review ended with a written report detailing substantive points covered in the review session and what the student was aiming to achieve before the next profiling session. This was written by the student, signed by both the student and the tutor and then filed in the student's portfolio. The discussions were usually sharply focused on the student's work by the use of the assignment sheets. The tutor's work was supplemented by the other members of the course team who would discuss with the students as a group each assignment as it came along, so helping the students with planning and evaluation.

Again the system was working fairly well because of the dedication of the tutor and the team approach of the course team. An advantage seemed to be that since one person was looking after all the students they had been able to develop an overview of all the students' progress which could be confirmed by discussions during course team meetings. The negotiation of student access to learning support was also easier and staff who were less confident about the action planning process than the tutor were able to concentrate on their subject teaching rather than on action planning.

Again though there was an element of stop and start and getting ready for the reviews, with large amounts of paper-filling, was often seen as a chore by the students. None the less most of the portfolios of work were being well maintained and the students seemed to have a clear idea of what they were trying to achieve before the next review though they were better able to describe their weaknesses rather than their strengths. The tutor did feel that she was unable to spend enough time with each student and she wanted the amount of time with individual students increased, especially at the beginning of the course. The course team were exploring ways that this could be achieved but none of them doubted the value of this additional tutorial time.

Case Study 3: An organic solution

This school had recognised the central importance of action planning from the beginning and because of their history and involvement in TVEI (Technical and Vocational Education Initiative) many staff had experience of approaches involving much tutorial work. In addition to regular reviews which occurred every half term and were largely concerned with paperwork and making sure portfolios were being maintained, students had access to tutorial support whenever they needed it and with whom they needed it. Such tutorials might last just a few minutes to clear up a misunderstanding or longer if the tutor was reviewing a piece of work with a student or going over plans for a particular assignment. This freedom was achieved by adopting an almost entirely workshop-based approach to the GNVQ course with students working individually or, more usually in small groups, on projects. The teachers then used their time to support the work or in giving tutorials.

Records of these meetings were kept by students who were entering them in their portfolios as evidence to count towards the grading criteria. The advantage here was that students were being given help when they needed it and the help was being directed to those who needed it most. The problem had been in convincing the students to work in this way and not see asking for help as being a sign of weakness. This had been accomplished during the induction phase and through continued monitoring of pupil work as it was handed in, marked, returned with comments and then discussed in these impromptu tutorials. The students had rapidly realised that by taking the initiative in asking for help they were going to get the best out of the system.

Again the system was working well because of the team approach of the staff and the fact that they had developed this system and therefore felt they owned it. Other staff within the same institution were sometimes aghast at what they considered to be its haphazard nature but it worked for these staff and for these students.

Furthermore the students felt they were equal partners because they could initiate the tutorial discussions rather than just being summoned for a tutorial at a set time.

Conclusion

All of these approaches have their advantages but they worked because the staff were committed to the idea of action planning, of helping the students to make progress through talking about their achievements and planning for the future. Each system had been thought out, everyone, including the students, understood the rationale behind what they were doing and they realised the importance of action planning to achieving the higher grades on the GNVQ. Indeed records of the action-planning sessions were being used by students in all three institutions to support their claims for merits and distinctions for their portfolios of work. The process also ensured that the weaker students' needs were continually being monitored and discussed with them so that students were going to seek help with their work from the learning support systems not because they had been told to but because they realised the need.

These institutions were however special in the sense that they were already running similar types of programme within existing qualifications, e.g. BTEC National, or they were committed to a particular view of teaching because of their history, e.g. as a TVEI school. I would not suggest that any of these systems will be appropriate to your institution. Indeed, you may have no choice about the action-planning system you use but I do hope it has given you some ideas about the sorts of things you might do in an action-planning session, and how you might begin to convince those who decide such things how your system might be changed if it is not working to help you with your students.

Bibliography

Bees, M and Sword, M (1990) *National Vocational Qualifications and Further Education*, London: Kogan Page.

BTEC (1993a) *Implementing BTEC GNVQs: A Guide for Centres*, London: BTEC.

BTEC (1993b) *GNVQ2 and GNVQ3 Business*, London: BTEC.

City & Guilds (1993) *GNVQ Handbook*, London: City & Guilds.

DES (1991) *Education and Training for the 21st century, Volume 2: The challenge to colleges*, London: HMSO.

Department of Employment (1993) *A Year in GNVQ 1992/93: The School Perspective,* Sheffield: Employment Department.

FEU (1993a) *Core Skills Action Pack*, London: FEU.

FEU (1993b) *Managing Learning*, London: FEU.

FEU (1994) *Planning Co-ordinating and Managing the GNVQ Curriculum*, London: FEU.

Jessup, G (1991) *NVQs and the Emerging Model of Education and Training*, London: Falmer Press.

NCVQ (1993a) *NCVQ Information Note: General National Vocational Qualifications*, London: NCVQ.

NCVQ (1993b) *Assessing Core Skills in GNVQ,* London: RSA.

Ollin, R and Tucker, J (1994) *The NVQ and GNVQ Assessor Handbook,* London: Kogan Page.

PSSI (1993) issue 12, Association for Science Education.

Royal Society of Arts (1993a) *Business Intermediate and Advanced GNVQs*, RSA: Coventry.

Royal Society of Arts (1993b) *GNVQ Centre Guidelines*, Coventry: RSA.

Royal Society of Arts (1993c) *Unit Tests Specifications*, Coventry: RSA.

Wolfe, A. (1993) *Assessment Issues and Problems in a Criterion-based System*, London: FEU.

Index

accreditation of prior learning (APL) 132, 141–2
achievement recording 68–9
  see also evidence of achievement
Action Plan 177, 181
action planning
  advice from awarding bodies 175–9
  case studies 179–88
  cyclical approach 186–7
  importance of 179
  language of 177
  organic solution 187–8
  rationale 176
  review sessions 175
  role of 176
  teachers in 177
Action Planning Sheet 66
activities, range of 36
additional core skill units 19, 87, 96–7
additional support 99, 133
administrative system 83
Advanced GNVQ 32, 45, 95
  student enrolment 161–2
Application of Number core skill units 114–21
  performance criteria 116
  range statements 116–18
  staff responsibility 120–21
  subject knowledge 118–20
  themes and elements 116
  vocational contexts and learning 115–16
assessment 49–78
  advance planning 137
  approaches to 138
  basic considerations 128–9
  case study 58–70
  complexity 49
  core skills 137–42
  cyclical process 57
  internal continuous 56–8
  model of 56
  nature of 49
  new methods 50
  ongoing 138
  overview 50–52
  performance criteria 67–8
  planning 55, 58, 138
  retrospective 138
  stages of 56
  student involvement 54, 65
  student planning for 63–4
  types of assessment 50
Assessment Activity Action Plan 64
assessors 27
assignment activity action plan 85
assignment cover sheet 69, 85
assignments 34, 37
  action planning 64–5
  case study 60–62
  core skills in 137–8
  desirable features 82–3
  induction 174–5
  model 80
  organising the students 62–3
  published schemes 80–82
  referral process 68
  student briefing 64
  student planning 63–4
  verification 68–9
  writing 79–83
awarding bodies 15
  guideline documentation 129

collaboration need 47–8
Communication core skill units 102–14
  elements of achievement 102–3
  implications for teaching 112
  performance criteria 103–7
  progression and differentiation 112–13
  range statements 107
  requirements of 102
  staff responsibility 113–14
  themes 102
competence 33–4
complex activities 75–6
constraints on teaching 30
core skill implementation
  ad hoc approach 132–3
  assignments or specific tasks 133
  strategic approach 130–32
core skill units 16, 17, 20, 87
  familiarisation with 89–90
  language of 94
  specification 90–92
  student involvement implications 95–6
core skills 19–21
  assessment 137–42
  course team 136
  in assignments 137–8
  status of 135–6
  talking about 136
  transferability 98–9
course delivery 97–9
  case studies 99–101
course development 48
course team 26–7, 27, 48, 58, 130
  core skills 136
  in review sessions 149
  in student learning 145–8
course tutor 27
  as personal tutor 148

discrete tasks 75–76
distinction 70–78
documentation 85, 86

elements of achievement 21–3, 32–4
  communication core skill units 102–3
evidence of achievement 37, 52–6, 98
  authenticity 52–4
  indicators of 21, 25–6, 39
  methods of generating and assessing 54
  notion of 26
  types of 53, 54
  validity of 54, 139
  variety of 53
  see also portfolio of evidence
external tests 40, 51–2
  marking 51–2
external verifier 27

feedback provision 140
focus 42–3
Foundation GNVQ 45, 95
  student enrolment 159
Further Education Unit (FEU) 145

GNVQs
  aim of 14–15
  areas covered 8
  comparison with NVQs 15
  definition 14–16
  employment outcome 14
  numbers of units currently available 16
  overview 13–29
  pilots 8
  specification 7
  structure of 16–17, 171
  uniqueness 13
  unit-based qualifications 16
  see also Advanced GNVQ; Foundation GNVQ; Intermediate GNVQ
grading 70, 70–78
  criteria 26, 71–5
  problems of 70
  themes 70–71

induction 167–75
  assignment approach 174–5
  block of time approach 172–3
  familiarisation procedures 171–2
  importance of 167
  introducing the course 171
  models of 172–5
  programmes 167–8
  rationale 168–9
  student handbook approach 173–4
  student–teacher relationship 171
information flow 84, 86
Information Technology core skill units 121–5
  performance criteria 122–5
  range statements 122–5
  themes and elements 122
inputs 33
Intermediate GNVQ 45, 95
  student enrolment 160–61
internal verifier 27
internally devised test 52

Jessup, Gilbert 33

knowledge application 93–4
knowledge categories 43
knowledge statements 42–3

learning outcomes 33
learning process, basic considerations 128–9
learning programme 35, 38
learning skills 47
learning support system 133
learning support workshop 133
levels of attainment 8, 16, 91–2

mandatory core skill units 24, 87, 91, 95, 102–27
  integration with vocational units 125–30
mandatory vocational units 17–19
mapping 126–7
merit grade 70–78
monitoring 27
multiple choice items 51

National Record of Achievement 170, 175

ongoing assessment 138
optional units 19
outputs 34

paperwork management 69, 83–6, 149–50
pass grade 70
pass requirements 17
performance criteria 21, 23–5, 32–4, 36, 42
  Application of Number core skill units 116
  assessment process 67–8
  Communication core skill units 103–7
  design proposals 125–6
  Information Technology core skill units 122–5
  satisfying 139–40
performance evidence 53, 54
personal skills 87
personal tutor 27, 147
  course tutor as 148
  in student learning 148–50
  qualities required 149
  relationship with students 149
portfolio index 85, 183
portfolio of evidence 55–6
  assessing material 67
  collecting material 65
  managing paperwork 69
  skills required 75
portfolio of work 34, 39
pre-course counselling
  impact on students 165
  initial contact with student 158
pre-enrolment counselling 162–3
  case study 163–6
  undecided students 164–5
problem solving core skill unit 87

progression 141

quality-enforcing body 15

range statements 21, 25, 38–40
  Application of Number core skill units 116–18
  Communication core skill units 107
  Information Technology core skill units 122–5
record-keeping 84, 85, 140–41, 187
resource requirements 129
retrospective assessment 138
review sessions 147–8
  action planning 175
  course team in 149
  planning 150
review sheet 184

skills needed 47
staff responsibilities 26–7
  Application of Number core skill units 120–21
  Communication core skill units 113–14
staff roles 26–7
standards 33, 34
student aspirations 157–8
student characterisation 158–62
student enrolment 156–62
  Advanced GNVQ 161–2
  Foundation GNVQ 159
  implications 95–6
  initial contact 158
  Intermediate GNVQ 160–61
  reasons for increases in 157
  see also pre-enrolment counselling
student handbook 173–4
student learning
  active management of 145–55
  case studies 151–5
  course teams in 145–8
  induction role 169–71
  management of 143–4
  model 145–8
  personal tutor in 148–50
  teacher's role in 148
student–teacher partnership 165–6
student–teacher relationship, induction 171
supplementary evidence 53, 54

teacher, problems of 36
teachers 27
  in action planning 177
  role of 36
  in student learning 148
teaching implications 34–7
teaching methodology 28, 30–34
  basic considerations 128–9
teaching syllabus 28
test specifications 32, 38, 40–46
testing 51–2
  planning 51
time requirements 129
tracking documents 183
tracking sheet 181, 182
Training Development Lead Body (TDLB) 56
transferability problem 134–6
  bridging for 134–5
TVEI (Technical and Vocational Education Initiative) 187

understanding, application of 93–4
unit
  concept of 28
  definition 17
  structure of 22
  terminology 21
  types of 16, 17, 17–21
unit code 21
unit specifications 32, 33, 39–40, 45, 89
unit title 21

vocational units 17
  mandatory core skills integration with 125–30